W9-ARC-573

How to Have
More Love
in Your Life

Also by Alan Epstein

How to Be Happier Day by Day

How to Have More Love in Your Life

Everyday Actions for Nourishing Heart and Soul

Alan Epstein, Ph.D.

Viking

VIKING
Published by the Penguin Group
Penguin Books USA Inc., 375 Hudson Street,
New York, New York 10014, U.S.A.
Penguin Books Ltd, 27 Wrights Lane,
London W8 5TZ, England
Penguin Books Australia Ltd,
Ringwood, Victoria, Australia
Penguin Books Canada Ltd, 10 Alcorn Avenue,
Toronto, Ontario, Canada M4V 3B2
Penguin Books (N.Z.) Ltd, 182–190 Wairau Road,
Auckland 10, New Zealand

Penguin Books Ltd, Registered Offices:
Harmondsworth, Middlesex, England

First published in 1994 by Viking Penguin,
a division of Penguin Books USA Inc.

1   3   5   7   9   10   8   6   4   2

Copyright © Alan Epstein, 1995
All rights reserved

Library of Congress Cataloging in Publication Data
Epstein, Alan.
How to have more love in your life: everyday actions for
nourishing heart and soul/Alan Epstein.
p.   cm.
ISBN 0–670–85445–X
1. Love—Problems, exercises, etc. 2. Intimacy
(Psychology)—Problems, exercises, etc. I. Title.
BF575. L8E5C   1995
158'.2—dc20
94–31392

Printed in the United States of America
Set in Century Book Condensed

Without limiting the rights under copyright reserved above, no part of this
publication may be reproduced, stored in or introduced into a retrieval system, or transmitted, in any form or by any means (electronic, mechanical,
photocopying, recording or otherwise), without the prior written permission
of both the copyright owner and the above publisher of this book.

For Diane, Julian, and Elliott
and for everyone
I've met along the way

Acknowledgments

Despite the many hours of solitary effort, a book is always a collective endeavor.

I'd like to thank my two wonderful families for their constant support and encouragement, and for providing Diane, me, and the kids with such a loving environment.

To my friends, thank you for showing me time and again how priceless and fulfilling friendships can be.

To my clients, I appreciate the responsibility you've entrusted me with to help bring more love into the world.

To my colleagues at Viking Penguin—Pam Dorman, Carolyn Carlson, Carolyn Coleburn, Susan Elia, Cathy Hemming, Paul Slovak—let me say that I continue to appreciate the confidence you have in my ideas, the considerable work that you do to get me to state them in the most eloquent manner possible, and the efforts you make to get the finished product disseminated far and wide.

To my agents Patti Breitman and Linda Michaels, thank you for your constancy, for your sound judgment, for sharing your knowledge of the world of books with me, and for being so much fun to work with.

To Deborah Dickson, thanks for your wonderful aesthetic sense and for creating covers which demonstrate that a book can also be a work of art.

To George Leonard, I am indebted to you for GRACE and for the comfort of "soft eyes" and the "long body."

To Julian and Elliott, my eternal appreciation for the

opportunity to be your father and for teaching me about love and forgiveness.

To Diane, *grazie mille* for being such an incomparable true partner and for your efforts, large and small, to help me be the person you always knew I was capable of being.

Contents

WINTER

Introduction

As a relationship counselor, seminar leader, speaker, and matchmaker, I am privy to the longing for love felt by a wide variety of people. Some arrive to see me with faith and exuberance, seeking to add to their already loving lives a partner with whom they can share that love. Others, however, arrive with unfulfilled or broken dreams—and often with aspirations, as yet unrealized, that they would like to incorporate into their lives through other people. They then judge their ability to "fall in love" or "be in love" on the basis of whether they are involved with partners who embody these aspirations.

By focusing their ability to experience love so narrowly on an intimate relationship between two people, these men and women often overlook how much love already or potentially exists in their lives—with or without an intimate partner. Moreover, they fail to see how much their search for a meaningful, intimate relationship can be aided by learning to love more truly and genuinely, by developing or deepening their relationships with the many aspects of life that energize human interaction or go beyond it.

How to Have More Love in Your Life is a practical guide to experiencing these relationships consciously so that you—whether you are married or single, in an intimate relationship, exploring your relationship with yourself, or merely trying to ask the right questions—can have more love in your life through your own efforts. The book assumes that love is active, not reactive, and that it does not depend on luck or external circumstances that are out of your control. Rather, it maintains that you are capable of cultivating love through attitudes you develop and actions you take in your everyday life. The book also assumes that the areas of your life you focus on will expand and enlarge, so that creating a loving life becomes a matter of concentrating on the opportunities around you that are conducive to love.

Everyone wants love, to love and be loved. But many people think that "true" love is more or less romantic love, and that it is a state of being relatively unconnected from other, more mundane relationships that characterize everyday life. But these other relationships can—with attention and dedication—provide the same sense of belonging, the same intensity of feeling, as romantic love. *How to Have More Love in Your Life* redefines love to encompass a fuller and more varied range of human behavior, and is intended for anyone who wants to have more love and who is willing to deliberately create that love through action. It maintains that love is the ability to connect, that the reward of love is empowering oneself with the ability to attract and engage wholeheartedly, and that anyone, including you, has the capacity to liberate love from the confines of infatuation, lust, obligation, and habit and to see loving possibilities in many places—inherent, in fact, in every moment.

How to Have More Love in Your Life looks at aspects of everyday life that are laden with loving possibilities. Having more love is a matter of charting and successfully navigating a course through areas of your life so that you can create and have love that derives from your attitudes and actions. While any of the aspects of everyday life I'll discuss can and will provide you with love if you mindfully focus on them, a deep and healthy relationship with all of them will create balance and harmony in your life, make each aspect that much more fulfilling, and enhance your ability to connect with and attract whatever you desire.

The aspects are as follows:

Getting Ready for Love—how to develop the attributes that can accelerate the arrival of intimate love in your life.

The Promise of Courtship and Commitment—how the process of developing a relationship with another person is itself an opportunity to find out about a life of love.

Intimacy and Communication for Couples—how intimate love for another person is a full expression of a loving life.

Setting the Imagination Aglow—how the often under-used power of the imagination fuels the process of bringing more love into your life.

Knowing Thyself—how a healthy relationship with your-self is the necessary foundation for all other loving relationships.

The Mystery of the Natural World—how immersion in the visible world encourages you to appreciate beauty, harmony, and the natural rhythms of life.

Deepening Friendship and a Sense of Community—how friends can constitute a dependable loving experience for you, and how being connected to a larger group enables you to reach beyond your personal world to a much larger one.

Feeding the Mind and Spirit—how delighting in learning allows you to transform your experience through openness, sensitivity, and patience, and how, through play, you can become more focused and joyful, two prerequisites for love.

The Pleasures of Work and Creative Self-Expression—how the satisfaction that work can provide goes far beyond task, job, or career, and results in a more passionate, prosperous way of life.

Family Lessons—how sound relationships with family members can enable you to become more loving through attention, acceptance, and forgiveness.

The Path of Healing and Wellness—how a balanced sense of mind, body, and spirit promotes openness and receptivity to loving possibilities, and how staying on a healthy path helps to focus on the love that already exists around you.

Encountering the Soul Through the Invisible World— how developing a relationship with what can't be seen is the true test of love and faith.

For every one of these aspects of everyday life, I suggest a number of actions you can take to deepen your relationships in that area. You'll see that the aspects of life are tied to particular seasons, to indicate that love, like everything else, has cycles, and in some cases my suggestions reflect these times of year. Since intimacy with another person is central to the experience of love, and since intimate life is different for couples than it is for single people, I have devoted separate sections to these experiences. There is also a section on courting, the process by which intimate love blossoms. I have coupled friendship and community, which seem naturally related to me, and combined learning and play under the heading "Feeding the Mind and Spirit."

I introduce each section with a brief essay that ties together the suggestions for that particular aspect of love. If you are familiar with my previous book, *How to Be Happier Day by Day: A Year of Mindful Actions,* you will recognize my tone and sensibility. Some of my suggestions are simple and direct—prepare a candlelit dinner, or spend time with a sibling. Others are more challenging— forgive someone, or discuss money with your partner. But I have tried to present the suggestions in an accessible manner and to write them in a way that will encourage you to attempt them, using instructions, examples, and personal anecdotes throughout. Some suggestions are fun and whimsical, others are more serious. Some are ideas for enriching your inner life, and others are for improving your connection to the outer world. All contribute to a greater understanding of how your attitudes and actions largely determine both the quality and quantity of love that you experience.

My view of love is based on the conviction that love is greater and more comprehensive than our normal definition of the word. While romantic love and all that is connected to intimacy can be integral parts of a loving life, they are by no means all of it. Some people have a great deal of love in their lives without having an intimate partner, and others who have a partner have little or no love. *How to Have More Love in Your Life* demonstrates how a life of love encompasses much more than intimate love, and how intimacy is enhanced and enriched by other kinds of successful relationships.

My objective throughout the book is to empower you to actively develop loving relationships—with yourself, your potential, your family and loved ones, the people with whom you come into contact on a daily basis, your work, the natural world, and the Invisible World. In developing and deepening these relationships, you will see many more possibilities for love than you did before, and be encouraged to act on them. In turn, you will create a more nourished heart and soul—for yourself and for others.

How to Use This Book

How to Have More Love in Your Life
can be used in a variety of ways. You can:

1. follow each suggestion, day by day and section by section, as a systematic way of increasing your potential for love
2. concentrate on the elements you feel are most important for you, skipping others
3. work on a suggestion in a different season from the one in which it is presented, or change the order of suggestions within a particular section
4. attempt a suggestion from each of the sections on consecutive days
5. refer to the book when you feel in need of inspiration, motivation, or guidance
6. discuss the suggestions with people in your life who mean a lot to you, or form a support group and choose one or more aspects to concentrate on together.

As with suggestions from anyone, only do what feels comfortable to you, especially with the section "The Path of Healing and Wellness." Please consult your physician if you are under medical care for a specific condition. But also try some suggestions to which at first you are resistant. Often, something that prompts a strong reaction involves an issue that you may need to look at more closely. If you have great discipline and a tremendous capacity to work but have difficulty playing, you might first want to look at

"The Pleasures of Work and Creative Self-Expression" to get an idea of the kinds of activities I have in mind in an area in which you are comfortable before moving on to the suggestions contained in "Feeding the Mind and Spirit." If your relations with your family couldn't be better but you have a hard time connecting with people in an intimate way, you still may want to look at "Family Lessons" before turning to "Getting Ready for Love." There may be something you have overlooked in your dealings with family members that could offer an insight into your difficulty with strangers or potential partners.

Of course, if you have a strong desire to get more love out of your work, or are experiencing issues with your intimate partner that need immediate attention, by all means go directly to these sections and jump right into them. If you want to deepen your love in any way possible, just start with Day One in Spring and go through the book suggestion by suggestion. The result will be a life of greater integration, balance, and harmony.

How to Have
More Love
in Your Life

Spring

Getting Ready for Love

The primary issue for people who have difficulty forming or maintaining an intimate relationship is not the inability to find someone to love but their own ambivalence about loving. They may say they want to be involved, but a part of them ranges all the way from somewhat reluctant to outright terrified, and it is this part of their psyche that somehow prevents them from connecting.

Ultimately, ambivalence cannot be wished away. The part of you that has doubts and fears, that does not see yourself possessing the inner resources to be successful in an intimate relationship, cannot be made to disappear by convincing yourself that it doesn't exist. These doubts and fears can only be overcome through action, through practice, by allowing yourself to go forward with love in spite of your reservations, hesitations, frustrations, difficulties, irritations, and apprehensions. The courage to act, to take risks, to be vulnerable does not come from making a clear path in life and then walking down the middle of it. It comes from taking action in spite of your fears.

Going ahead with love does not mean pretending that you could be involved with every person you meet. Nor does it mean holding on to a relationship that doesn't work for you, in which there isn't enough compatibility to enable you to see yourself maturing together. It does mean that *you look to connect,* rather than looking for any reason not to. It means accepting another person's foibles because you have a realistic understanding of your own, and not allowing an unrealistic sense of perfectionism to stop you from proceeding.

People are either ready for love or they are not. Although your readiness level may be higher or lower, once you start to fall on the low side it's very difficult to create a loving relationship, because your ambivalence is preventing you from seeing yourself with *anybody.* If you're looking to find a reason not to pursue a potential relationship with someone, you'll find it. Even couples who have been together happily for years can regale you with tales of the times their spouses drove them crazy.

That's what a good relationship is—a challenge, an opportunity to grow, to explore your differences, to see yourself anew because the changing nature of the entire universe is represented in this perfect stranger you have chosen to go through life with and in this third entity that the two of you have created together called your relationship. It's a living, changing, dynamic, mysterious thing, and people who have gone on to build a successful one, even after a whirlwind romance in which they found themselves madly in love, will tell you that what counts is not the sexual passion, the knockout good looks, the second home in the country, or the kid's private school.

No, what counts are qualities more amorphous and sublime: the quality of respect—for yourself and for your partner—and the ability to listen, to allow your mate to express himself or herself fully and to encourage your mate to do so freely. What counts is love, not merely passion, not merely romance, and not the smug satisfaction of how good-looking or successful your partner is, but the sense of reaching out, of support, kindness, consideration, generosity, and regard.

Those who look to their partners to solve all their problems, to make everything all right for them, to save their lives in some way, will be devastated with disappointment when time wears away the romance and the reality of day-to-day life with another person takes over. Those who understand the difference between love and romance do well in relationships, because together they can build a life based in truth and authenticity.

$D_{ay\ one}$ Examine your ideas about romance. See if you understand the difference between love in the unfolding of a real relationship in real life and the unreal dream you've seen in movies and read about in novels. Can your ideas about romance withstand the scrutiny of reality? Are you looking for someone to rescue you because you cannot find fulfillment on your own? Are you looking for a person with qualities you don't think you possess? Scroll through your past and see if you have tried to project onto a potential partner requirements that no human could possibly live up to.

Go over in your mind the qualities you would like to see in a partner, your list of requirements. Are they realistic? Do they reflect the person you are on the inside? Are you too concerned with the wrapping and not concerned enough with the gift? Are you aware that a person can change her hair color, shave off his beard, get a whole new wardrobe, get manicures, learn to ride a motorcycle, study Portuguese, and institute a variety of changes on the outside but rarely make the changes on the inside that would make his or her values similar to yours?

When you examine your myths about romance, you may better understand why connecting with someone has not been easy. Perhaps you are too focused on the Hollywood version of love and not focused enough on the Peoria version. Is your own inner life sufficiently developed to handle the inevitable rough spots that emerge in any intimate relationship? Can you see yourself possessing the qualities you admire so much, so that gaining them through someone else is not so crucial to you?

Love is real; it isn't phony. Love is enduring; it isn't here today and gone tomorrow. Love is patient; it doesn't insist right now. What can you do to reevaluate your notions of love and romance?

Day two Be open to every encounter. Have no preconceived ideas about love, or about your mate. Although many of us like to imagine meeting our true partner "across a crowded room," most significant relationships start in a way that cannot be predicted, or even imagined. What's important is to allow whatever wants to unfold to in fact do so, to not close off possibilities simply because you haven't thought of them.

I am certainly not suggesting here that you try to read into every interaction something that might not be there, or think that everyone you meet is ripe for a meaningful relationship with you. What I am saying is that possibilities for love occur at the oddest moments, often when you least expect them to, and having a preconceived notion of who your partner is going to be and how you are going to meet him or her can slow down the process, and even have you looking in the wrong places.

If a friend wants to introduce you to someone or have you meet a lovely person at your company picnic, or if you suddenly find yourself engaged in a lively conversation with a perfect stranger over cappuccino in a local café, be receptive to the possibility. It could be more significant than you think.

Being open to every encounter optimizes your chances of finding someone special. You are telling the universe that you don't know how your true partner will come into your life, only that you are asking for the perfect person to appear at the perfect time—whoever and whenever that is.

Day three   Make a candlelit dinner for one—yourself. Go through the entire process as if you were preparing a meal for a special occasion for you and your lover. For some single people this is the most difficult thing imaginable, to lovingly prepare a meal as if someone else were there. But the benefits of doing this are manifold.

Go ahead, do it right. Carefully prepare the menu. Select the foods you like, and imagine what your partner would want to eat as well. Buy flowers as you shop for the ingredients to prepare your special repast. If you are feeling particularly courageous, you can even set another place at the table, the one for your partner—the man or woman who will be coming into your life shortly. Savor every aroma as your spinach-and-ricotta lasagne or grilled swordfish cooks to perfection. Put on your favorite romantic music and really create an atmosphere that is irresistible and inviting.

Take your time. Don't rush through things. Draw out the evening so that you treat yourself the way you would treat your lover. Dress up for the occasion and light two candles, one for you and one for your partner-to-be. Imagine him or her there with you, sharing the result of your loving attention, the delicious flavors of the various dishes you have prepared.

Don't feel compelled to clean up after your meal. Act the way you would if your lover were there with you. Listen to more music, curl up with a fabulous book, or watch a romantic movie, all the while trying to conjure up the presence of your partner, almost as if you could make him or her materialize by the sheer force of your imagination.

Day four   Think about the best relationship you ever had. Even if it wasn't perfect, or had serious flaws, or ended sadly, or wasn't quite compelling enough to endure, think about what worked, why you were involved with this person, what it meant to you, what you learned from the experience, and how it changed you. If you've never had a significant relationship, think about any relationship—with a friend, a close relative, someone you work with—and consider the aspects of your connection that pleased you and lingered with you.

Having love in the present or future means building on what worked in the past. To have a clear picture of what your next relationship will consist of, think back to a time when you were happy with someone. What did that feel like? What were the conditions or circumstances that contributed to your enjoyment? Were you college sweethearts? Did you share an interest in saving the world and stay up many nights talking about all the things you would improve if only you had the opportunity?

Or was your best relationship with a man in Chicago you met on an extended business trip? Was the excitement you and he shared directly related to knowing that your moments together would be brief? Was your overwhelming attraction fueled by the mutual understanding that your relationship was limited by time and space? See if you can imagine yourself building on all the qualities of the past that worked, all the qualities that were as close as you've ever come to having what you wanted.

Try to recall how you were with this person, what your life felt like. Did you make elaborate meals together? Did you take wonderful trips to interesting places? Or was it the way she was with the people in her life, her patience and understanding, that made you feel special just knowing her? Keep in mind that other people possess the qualities that you admired. No one, of course, shares all the characteristics in exactly the same way, but kindness, sexiness, intellectual prowess, and honesty are more prevalent in people than you might think. If you were around it before, you are likely to be around it again if you uphold these qualities as the standards by which you live your own life.

$\mathcal{D}$ay five   Become aware of the messages you give off. All of us are constantly sending signals—some conscious and others unconscious—about who we are and who we'd like to be with.

Many of us are unaware of how real communication takes place between people. So much of what is said is somehow spoken between the words themselves. For instance, when you're talking to someone, more than half of the way in which you are being perceived is by the way you look—the way you dress, your mannerisms, gestures, posture, and so on. Another big chunk is the tone of your voice—its decibel level, modulation, inflection, and so forth. Only a fraction of what you're communicating is actually the meaning of the words you are uttering. It makes sense, then, to like the way you look and sound, or to work on accepting your looks if changing them seems like too big a step for you right now.

Make sure your messages are clear and consistent. If you want to attract an undeniably attractive person, do what you can to optimize your own attractiveness, since that's merely what he or she is doing. Pay closer attention to the way you dress. Is your appearance neat and clean? If not, are you prepared to be with someone for whom that doesn't matter? Is that the person you want to attract?

Do you see yourself as an intelligent, thoughtful person who has interesting things to say (at least most of the time) but suspect that others find you preachy, tedious, and tiresome? Perhaps you're giving off the wrong message. Learn to moderate your speech. Use qualifiers. Say "I think" and "It's my impression that" rather than appearing to be certain all the time. Throw out ideas as suggestions, rather than certainties. Ask what others think of your opinions. Consider whether your air of apparent certainty masks an underlying insecurity, and whether this inconsistency means there's work to be done internally.

At first, thinking about your demeanor may seem like an extra burden, merely another thing to worry about when you're getting ready for love and trying to be your best. But in time, with practice, you will understand what you are communicating to people. Solicit feedback from friends and acquaintances. Find out what they think about you. Ask them to be honest and candid in their appraisal. And offer to do the same for them, whether they are attached or unattached. There are many areas in life in which we can become more aware of our signals.

$\mathcal{D}$ay six   Make a "dream board" of your relationship with your partner-to-be. Cut out a bunch of pictures, words, sayings, and other representations from magazines or other colorful sources and assemble a collage of your future relationship. Now paste what you've put together in such a way that it demonstrates—graphically—who you are and who you want to be with.

Many people have difficulty forming a relationship because they don't have a clear and vivid picture in their minds of what the relationship looks like. It's as if you're looking for something but you don't know what it is. A dream board will help you "see" what you're after. It will enable you to imagine this wonderful new relationship you are helping to bring into being. Keep in mind that most magazine pictures are of models, so be aware of the *feelings* portrayed in the images rather than the looks of the specific people. And remember that the purpose here is to help you focus on what you want your relationship to be like, not to limit yourself narrowly to what's on your board.

Relationships serve different functions for different people. Do you want to live lavishly with your partner, with a big house, exotic vacations, a fancy car, and elegant clothes? Find pictures of these images, cut them out, and group them together. Or do you want to live simply, in a small cottage with a lovely garden, with two cats and a fireplace in a country setting? Put that scenario together pictorially. Or do you dream of having both, to live simply in some respects, and lavishly in others?

Whatever you desire, it's important to affirm it by suffusing and surrounding yourself with images, settings, and words that convey the messages fully. Look at your dream board as often as you can. Absorb the content and especially the essence. See yourself and your partner-to-be romping on the beach on the Amalfi Coast, or sitting quietly in the backyard as your small children play contentedly beside you. It's yours for the asking.

Day seven   Treat yourself to something special.
So much of the joy of being in love involves feeling good
about giving and receiving. If you give yourself a gift, regardless of how big it is or how much it costs, you will be
telling yourself and the universe that you deserve to be
treated well. This in turn will increase the likelihood that
your relationships will be filled with generosity of heart.

Get some body work done—a facial or massage. Give
yourself an extra flair with the paisley shirt or scarf you
saw in a shop window on a recent stroll through your
neighborhood. Make the garment a part of your life, as
you savor the fact that you can appreciate yourself the
same way you can appreciate others—especially one other
person.

Take a trip to the country if you live in the city, or
vice versa. Spend the day shopping for unusual antiques
or going to a crafts fair, or taking in the smells, sights, and
sounds of a path through the woods far from the commo-
tion and crowds of the urban scene. See how much you
can do for yourself. Try to go beyond what you think of as
your limits to a higher level of indulgence. Rent a moped
and feel the wind on your face. Or stay in a luxury hotel
for a night and order room service. If your budget requires
something more modest, visit a museum and buy postcards
of the works or exhibits that appeal to you.

However you choose to give yourself a treat, learn to
make a habit of it. You will be sending a twofold

message—that you expect to be treated this way by others and that you are prepared to cherish others the way you cherish yourself. Start today.

Day eight   Have faith. This is perhaps the most difficult thing for an unattached person to work on, but it is also perhaps the most important. Having faith inoculates you from feeling desperate and demoralized, and allows you to maintain your appeal in spite of what may be the circumstances of your life.

Faith means knowing that it's just a matter of time before you are in a fulfilling relationship. It also means being aware that you can only do so much to influence the course of your life, that you also have to learn to let go of the outcome and trust that the right person will appear at the right time. The corollary to this is that you never know when that time is right. But you can always maintain your faith, in your ability to be clear about who you are and who you're looking for, and in the depth and quality of your character. Having faith also means leaving room in your life for another person to enter it.

Faith is also being specific about your requirements, knowing what's important in your life and what is not. It is knowing that you are blessed with talents, abilities, ex-periences, and a certain point of view that is unique to you, and that regardless of the fact that not everyone is going to appreciate who you are, someone will. I once heard Leo Buscaglia say that he was a delicious peach, and that not everyone liked peaches. Faith is waiting patiently for the person who does, doing what you can do, and letting other forces do their part also.

From my vantage point as a professional matchmaker, it's clear that the people easiest to help are the ones who have faith, who know that they are special and deserve to be with someone special, and that it's just a matter of time before that person arrives. This doesn't mean being passive, doing nothing, or giving up control to an omniscient, omnipotent presence. It does mean understanding the process of major life change—that almost everyone requires preparation before this can occur, that there are lessons to be learned while you are waiting for something you have affirmed to take place, and that if you don't learn them, you will be forced to learn your lessons again and again until you do.

Day nine   Smile. You'd be surprised at how much faster it is to make love happen in your life when you make a habit of this simple physical process. For a variety of reasons, smiling makes you happier and more open and gives you the appearance of being approachable, touchable, and lovable, the very qualities you are looking to develop in order to lead a loving life.

You can choose which people you want to smile at, or decide to take a small risk and smile randomly or at everyone for a day. Even if most others do not return your overture, you have benefited. And of course, it's always nice to smile at animals.

You can practice right now. See how much better your face feels when your mouth turns up and into a big grin. Smiling does wonders for your overall mental and emotional health as well. It stimulates the production of endorphins and relaxes the muscles in your face, which makes you feel better.

A line from an old song says it best: "When you're smiling, when you're smiling, the whole world smiles with you." Think about the people you know who have a lot of love in their lives and recall whether they smile a lot. I bet they do. Try to be one of them.

Day ten   Let go of having a certain "type." Fundamentally, there is no "type." Stop thinking you will only date redheads, or guys with beards, or someone with an MBA, or women who are under 5'6", or men over 6'. Of course there are people to whom you are attracted and those to whom you are not, but considering them as a "type" obscures their individuality, so that you're really not seeing them.

Be open to individuals. Recognize that each man or woman is unique and has qualities and characteristics that no other person possesses. If you look at people this way, you will discover a wealth of romantic possibilities that you never knew existed. But if you disqualify people based on superficial characteristics that can often be changed—as quickly as overnight—you are missing potential opportunities to meet your partner.

When people get stuck—with anything—it usually begins in their thinking. They are looking at the world in a certain way, and then lo and behold the world starts to conform to this way of thinking. "Type"-casting potential partners is a dangerous thing to do if you are serious about finding your true partner. It could mean that you deep down don't want to be involved with a real person in a real way. If you persist in this thinking, you are destined to end up like Charlie Brown, who knows he will be at the airport when his ship comes in.

Day eleven   Make a videotape of yourself. You can do this in your living room with a simple handheld camera and a tripod. If you don't already own a camera, you can either rent or borrow one, or if you think you might continue to use it, buy one. Many people don't see themselves as others see them, and if you're looking to have more love in your life, it's a good idea to have a general sense of how you appear. Making a tape of yourself is a good place to start.

First, get comfortable. Sit on your couch or in your favorite chair and have a conversation with your video camera. You need only do this for a few minutes. You'll get lots of good insight into yourself without having to recite the Gettysburg Address. The important thing is to relax and have fun. Pretend you are being interviewed by Larry King or Barbara Walters after having made an important scientific discovery, and now you're explaining to the entire country how you came up with this new theory. Or perhaps you just won the Oscar for Best Actress and you're basking in the bright light of recognition. Or talk about yourself the way you normally do.

When you've finished recording, you can watch what you've taped right away, but it's also a good idea to wait a while before looking at it so that your perspective on yourself is fresh. What's it like to see yourself on the screen? Do you look and sound the way you thought you did, or are you someone else entirely? Check out your reactions with friends or colleagues. Tell them your observations and see if they have reactions similar to yours. If the way you've thought of yourself and what you saw on tape are substantially different, see if you can evaluate your relationship history in this light. What changes, if any, do you have to make to become the person you want to be?

Day twelve Make love a priority. I'm often shocked when I meet people who are looking to have more love in their lives and who do almost nothing to make this blessing happen. Like anything else, love materializes when it is paid attention to, when it becomes the organizing principle of your life. It just doesn't happen to people who don't make room for it. It only appears when and where it is welcome, where there is intention and action.

The shorthand for all this is to be available. Support your intention with action. The first and easiest thing to do is to inform everyone in your life that you are serious about being in a committed relationship. It's the same as looking for a job. Let the world know. Second, follow up on every lead. Let no potential meeting go without some kind of inquiry. Who is she? Has he been married before? If so, how many times? What's the children situation? How often does she see them? Does he want any more? Find out all you can about this person before you go out with him or her. If you first meet at the Laundromat or at a party, and you can't find out too much before your assignation, then agree to get together for coffee in the afternoon at a public place.

If a friend or associate gives you the name and phone number of someone he or she thinks you ought to meet, make the call. If you're a woman and you prefer to be called, that's fine, too. Just let that be known. Spend a few minutes on the phone getting to know this man or woman, but keep in mind that great initial conversations are no guarantees of a fifty-year relationship. You're going to know a lot more about this person when you finally meet.

If you enjoy your time together at all, agree to meet again. This doesn't mean you have to start alerting your priest, minister, or rabbi, only that you want to spend more time together. If you're not sure, that's okay, too. Tell the other person to call you, or volunteer to call him, but if you do say you'll do this, at least make the call. It's so much more honorable, so much more dignified and noble to let someone else know what you're thinking, if you sense any interest on his or her part, than to keep the other person guessing. Many people think it's better to lie about their lack of interest than to hurt someone's feelings. Nothing could be less true. In Chinese, the ideogram for truth is a person standing next to his word.

If you make love a priority, you give the universe—which is nothing more than the universe of possibilities—the message that you are serious about your desire to be with a partner.

Day thirteen   Neutralize the past. The last thing you want to do is allow what happened to you before to interfere with the present, so it's important to see the past in at least a neutral light. This doesn't mean ignoring what has happened to you. If your romantic history has had setbacks, if you feel you haven't been lucky in love, it's important to start there. It won't help to pretend that what happened didn't happen, or that it didn't affect you in any way. Denying the past doesn't help you neutralize it.

At the same time, if you want to move ahead and have the most love you can right now, it's important to see your past in a positive light, and that means *interpreting what*

happened as a learning experience. Carrying around images of repeated failures will only predispose you to failure
in the future. If you've had a history of relationships with
women who were interesting but not dependable, or with
men who were handsome but not emotionally available, try
to see what you needed to learn from these people and
situations. Did choosing an unavailable partner reflect your
own ambivalence about being in a relationship? Were you
really ready to be involved then?

The past is your teacher, in a very real way the only
one you have. What has happened to you in no small part
has been your choice, even if you are not conscious of this.
By allowing yourself to participate in relationships that
didn't ultimately work, you were affording yourself the opportunity to learn something—even if it was unrelated to
the person or the relationship itself. If you chose people
who tended to be controlling, perhaps you needed to learn
how to assert yourself. If you chose men or women you
could dominate, perhaps giving up control was your issue.
Look to see how you changed as a result of the relationship, how differently you see yourself, other people, or life
in general.

Neutralizing the past is a healthy, positive way of cele-
brating your uniqueness, of understanding that whatever
your choices, you made them, and you are ultimately the
one who can learn from them.

The Promise of Courtship and Commitment

Many people approach dating warily. Stories about dates from hell abound, and many jokes about it are told by comedians and late-night talk-show hosts. I recently appeared on a television program to discuss dating after divorce, and one attractive woman in her thirties stood up and said that she didn't want to date at all, she just wanted to be married.

It's ironic that an activity that was so appealing to people when I was an adolescent has become so fraught with anxiety and negative connotations. Dating used to be seen as a natural and necessary part of the process of finding one's partner, and it still can be if you choose to see it as a means by which you determine if someone you're seeing has the potential to be your life mate.

Maybe part of the solution to this difficulty comes from changing the way we talk and think about it. If you view dating as the process of courtship, as a way for two people to reveal themselves to each other slowly and gradually build trust, respect, and love, then courtship can indeed be an edifying experience. It can lead naturally to commitment because the little acts and events that make up an enduring relationship are built into the very way you relate to each other from the beginning.

It's clear that you will not find everyone you date attractive or a potential true partner. But it's also clear that many people make judgments too hastily. They look for instant and unassailable proof that someone they've just met or are seeing for the first time is "the one." Before dating became so loaded with negative connotations, many successful relationships began when two people saw each other casually over time, either in the same class at school or when working together. Their everyday lives allowed them to get to know each other before any kind of formal date needed to take place.

Today's world seems so different from those times. People are in a hurry to have what they want. They often form idealistic or simply unrealistic visions of who they're looking for and even how they want to meet him or her. People often underestimate the power of courtship to introduce them not only to the charms of another but also to parts of themselves they never knew existed.

Dating does not have to be either a chore or a bore. If it threatens to become that, then something is wrong either with the things you're doing or the people you're seeing, or a combination of both. Courtship is a process of discovery, an opportunity to allow someone to enter your life slowly and naturally, and to allow you to enter his or hers. The moments you spend together are merely part of the process. Your times apart are just as important, for they too indicate what you are feeling, whether you miss the person you are seeing, whether you find yourself having little conversations with him throughout the day, or whether you are starting to make a mental list of anecdotes you can't wait to share.

Commitment is something many single people approach with the same kind of caution they would reserve for dealing with a boa constrictor. It's the proverbial "C-word." If your idea of commitment is marriage and family and her idea is seeing each other exclusively while the two of you live in separate households, then you either have to resolve your differences or find another partner.

Commitment is the ultimate test of one's ability to be fully present, to honor one's intention, to go no further than you want to but also to recognize that because no one promising seems to be coming along, making a halfhearted attempt at a relationship is not right. To be committed in mind, body, and spirit is the condition that allows you to experience what love for another person really feels like.

$\mathcal{D}ay\ one$ Take a risk. It doesn't have to be a big risk, although you may find that what seems to be risky now becomes no big deal when you try it. Whatever the magnitude of the risk, however large or small, take it today.

Your risk can involve the person you're seeing, or it can be limited to yourself. If there is someone in your Italian class that you've been exchanging pleasantries with and would like to know better, approach him. Say, *"Vuoi prendere un caffè"* in perfect Italian and see if he responds. Is there a miniskirt you've had your eye on for weeks but just haven't mustered up the courage to buy because it wouldn't be you? Do it. Break the mold. Be different. Wear it with confidence. Be someone you never thought you could be.

Love is not for the fainthearted or the meek. Love confers its rewards on those who reach out, who dare to grow, who are not complacently satisfied with the status quo. Having love in your life means that you are willing to take a chance, to do things differently. It means putting aside the safe and secure, risking your self-image, of even being willing to make a fool of yourself. Love loves fools.

Don't wait for another day. Don't put this off. Do it now. Call that woman you met at your friend's party. It doesn't matter that a month has passed. If she's going to respond to you, she'll respond whether a month or six months has gone by. Pick up the phone. The worst she can say is no, and maybe—just maybe—she's given you a thought or two since you met. You'll never know unless you risk it. And if she's not the one, at least you tried. Love not only loves fools, it also loves effort.

Day two   Bring a gift for your date. Something small and easy to obtain—like a bouquet, candy, or a bottle of wine—will do, but you can be even more creative if you really like the person you are seeing and want to demonstrate your creativity as well as your generosity.

Many people see dating as a way of finding out about someone else, and of course it is. But it is a way of revealing yourself as well, and greeting a date with a small but thoughtful gift is a way to show that you are different, that you take the time to acknowledge other people, that your partner can expect to be treated with love and generosity.

Even a card or a short note makes a difference. It can be fun to spend time picking out a card and writing just the right message to someone you've been having a good time with. You'll enjoy the initiative, he or she will enjoy receiving it, and your relationship will be marked by a spirit of giving.

Be careful not to overdo this. Dating doesn't require a gift every time you get together with someone. But if you do this judiciously, you'll find that people will want to spend more time with you.

Day three   See the movie *Groundhog Day*. It stars Bill Murray and Andie MacDowell, and it's both fun and instructive from beginning to end.

It's hard to think of a better movie when it comes to demonstrating the do's and don'ts of courting. If you don't know much about the movie, I'll give you a brief synopsis. A cynical, arrogant weatherman is forced to repeat the same day—Groundhog Day—which he is covering in the actual town, Punxsutawney, Pennsylvania, where the celebrated groundhog decides whether winter is over or has six weeks to go. This weatherman must relive this day over and over until he learns to have character. In the process, he must deal not only with his personal demons but also with his growing attraction for his producer, who has written him off as a jerk.

The story is about the moral development of this weatherman, who learns that the way to someone's heart is not through figuring out what the other person wants to hear and then saying it, but rather by developing one's own qualities and becoming more attractive by being a better person. It's a valuable lesson for everyone who wants to be loved and who wants to see how to be someone worth knowing.

Day four   Cook a meal together. This is probably not a good idea for a first date, but after a while, when you and the person you are seeing have spent some time together and know each other's tastes, it would be great to share a lunch or dinner that you yourselves have prepared.

Food plays a big part in courtship because it is such a major part of an intimate relationship. On my first date with my wife, I mentioned that I liked to cook. She asked what my specialties were, and I told her—Caesar salad, pasta *al pesto,* stuffed eggplant, and homemade tomato sauce. She said she liked every one of those, and her response was a welcome, encouraging one that was a harbinger of delicious meals we have eaten together over the years.

Start with the planning. You can volunteer to make your specialty, or decide to cook something neither of you has ever made but you both are eager to try. This is a good idea because you will see what it's like to work with your partner in the kitchen. Don't expect perfection, that you will smoothly and flawlessly work together with precision and minimum effort. Even Fred Astaire and Ginger Rogers practiced. Allow for the fact that one of you is working in a totally unfamiliar environment and may not know where to find the whisk.

You could decide to do something elaborate, but even simple dishes will suffice. Remember, the point here is to see how you work together, to explore new territory in your relationship, to reveal your respective creative abilities, and to have fun. Even if you have no feel for cooking, if it is not your forte, offer to be the sous chef, to do whatever the head of the kitchen asks of you.

When you sit down to eat, keep in mind that the meal may be your first joint creative effort and may prove to be the first of many. Smile across the table and offer a toast to a job well done.

*D*ay five   Learn to listen. So much of what makes a loving relationship loving is good communication, and so much of good communication is listening.

When you listen, do it actively. Halfhearted attempts are in many ways worse that not listening at all, since your partner believes you are listening. Pay careful attention. Try to hear what your partner is saying, and empty your mind of responses while he or she is talking. See if you can understand the feeling behind the words, the reason why he or she wants to communicate with you. Also see how it makes you feel, what gets triggered as you listen attentively.

When the woman you are seeing says, "While I'm flattered by your suggestion to go away for the weekend, I don't feel I'm ready for that," step back and absorb this. Do you take it as a personal rejection, or are you sensitive to her desire for more trust before proceeding? Can you hear the first part of her response as encouragement, or are you already trying to figure out how to change the second part?

Ask questions. Find out details. Clarify what you don't understand or what is unclear to you. You don't have to agree with everything the other person is saying. Being a good listener doesn't mean giving in when you don't want to. It means devoting all your energy to absorbing the essence of your partner's communication, of putting yourself in his or her position, of understanding his or her fear, joy, confusion, or desires. It's demonstrating that whatever else is going on with you, for the time the two of you are interacting nothing else matters.

The desire to listen is the most important skill in a successful relationship, the one thing you can rely on in difficult times. Learning to listen throughout your life—whether you are intimately involved or not—puts you on the path of love and understanding.

Day six Introduce your partner to your friends. If the man or woman you are seeing is going to be a permanent part of your everyday landscape, at some point he or she will have to fit into your social life. Go out with some of your friends and let them meet the person you are spending time with.

Sometimes a party or large gathering is the appropriate time to introduce this person, but a small dinner with no more than four other people might be an easier way to go. Try to do this at a restaurant so that neither you nor your date is concerned with getting the meal done just right. And make sure the place you choose is not too crowded or noisy and that you won't have to wait an annoyingly long time for a table.

See how the conversation goes. Remember, you are introducing a new person to old friends, so expect some new dynamics. What you are looking for is whether the meeting seems comfortable, how much your partner is interested in the topics of conversation, how friendly and responsive he or she is. Keep in mind also that this may be the first time the two of you are relating around people you know. Your own interaction may be different as well.

During the encounter, check in with your partner. I've seen situations like this one turn sour because someone felt abandoned or neglected. It's really up to you to integrate your partner and your friends so that your relationship is enhanced by the get-together.

There really is no one right time to do this. I met my wife's *mother* on our second date, and that was no problem for me at all. If your friends are good ones, and your partner is right for you, the mix will work out well for everyone.

Day seven Allow chemistry to develop. This might mean going out on a second date with someone you're not quite sure about. Or a third date. Or a fourth date, for that matter. The point here is not to disqualify a man or a woman as a potential partner because you are not struck by a bolt of lightning the first time you set eyes on him or her.

The chemistry between two people who fall in love doesn't necessarily manifest itself *completely* the first time they get together. It probably grows from a small kernel of compatibility into a much larger one, and that growth takes place over time, slowly, as both people begin to look for ways to connect with each other.

Many people pass up opportunities to explore relationships with people they could like because they don't allow chemistry to develop. They undertake the process of finding a mate with the mistaken notion that whatever is "there" between two people exists the moment they meet or not at all. In fact, with many couples, it's at first not present at all. Or it could even be disguised as hostility. Look at Beatrice and Benedek in Shakespeare's *Much Ado About Nothing.* They fight like cats and dogs before they realize the strength of their emotion comes from love, not hate. And what about the successful couples who know each other for months, sometimes years, before they decide to get involved romantically? This is the *process* of chemistry, of two people slowly revealing their charms over an extended period of time.

Give the person you're seeing a chance to reveal him- or herself in this manner. Two things will happen almost immediately. The first is that you will see how different someone can be every time you get together with him or her. The second is that people will start providing *you* with the opportunity to allow chemistry to develop. Now what could be better than that?

Day eight Don't be afraid to disagree about something. It could be a political matter, or something more personal. You could disagree about a movie. Or you could discuss your desire to move to the country, even though one of you loves the city.

I'm certainly not suggesting that you go out of your way to pick a fight with someone you like and met only a month ago. But I am saying that any relationship that takes root must be tested at some point by contention. Finding out early how you and your partner handle discord is a good indication of what you will face later on.

See how the disagreement progresses. Does it turn into a full-fledged argument? Are voices raised? Do you find yourself wondering why you are even seeing this person, or are you gaining more respect for him as you air your respective views? If you are debating a political matter, is your disagreement within your comfort zone of difference, or is it impossible for you to imagine being with someone who voted for Perot when you ardently supported Clinton?

What does it feel like to you to exchange views? Are you getting angry? Is your partner? Is the disagreement getting personal? Are you able to state your points completely, or are you being interrupted constantly? Do you find yourself interested in what your partner has to say?

Conflict between people, especially partners, is inevitable, and it makes sense to explore how conflict in your relationship will be resolved. If you criticize, even gently, something your partner said to a co-worker and she walks out, then you have learned a lot about how she will handle difficult situations with you. If your partner asks about your feelings, then you know immediately that he or she is open and interested in finding out who you are and how you can work to resolve contentious matters.

Day nine   Look to see what you can give, not what you can get. This is a good prescription for life in general, but it works especially well if you're trying to create more love through an intimate relationship.

If you are already a giving person, look for even greater ways to express your generosity. Unfortunately, most people who are seeking a relationship are usually trying to find someone who will give to them, not someone to whom they can give. They meet a man or woman and immediately start looking to see if the other person fulfills their requirements, not whether this person can appreciate their uniqueness and what they have to offer.

It all comes back to why people want to be involved, and most of the difficulty arises when people seek in a partner the qualities they lack. Another person can never supply what you don't have. If you're low-key and timid, you can't become outgoing and courageous by hooking up

with a live wire. You have to become more outgoing yourself. If you don't think your looks are so great, being with
a knockout won't make you any better-looking.

Love is something you get by giving it away. The more
you love, the more you *become* love, and an intimate relationship is a good place to practice. Look to see what
you can give—be it your intellectual ability, your tinkering
skills, your great talent in planning—and in time what you
give away will come back to you many times over.

It's easy to give, once you know how. Start today by
asking the person you're seeing how you can help him,
what you can do to ease his load—maybe listening to a
particularly perplexing problem and providing him with
your perspective. How attentive to her needs can you be?
What help can you extend? Does her friend who is coming
into town need a ride from the airport? Pick her up. Does
the sink in her bathroom drip? Replace the washer for her.
Is he having difficulty navigating his relationship with a
co-worker? See if you can shine an illuminating light on
the problem.

If you make giving a priority in your life and your relationship, you make yourself into a role model for your
partner, and you increase the likelihood of turning your
current relationship into an enduring one.

Day ten   Take love one step at a time. Many people make the mistake of going too fast, of trying to figure

it all out right away. Go slowly. Be patient. Learn to let love unfold.

Before you can meet and be with the love of your life, you first have to go out on a date. Look to find men or women who seem appropriate, whether you meet them on your own, through an introduction service or friends, or at a club. The first step is a date. Then, when you get together with him or her, keep in mind that the only purpose of this encounter is to see if you want to get together again. If you're sitting across the table from this person, having known him for ten minutes, trying to decide if he is the "right one," you'll not only drive yourself crazy, you really won't see him for who he is. You'll be lost in a world of who *you* are instead, and that won't help you evaluate the suitability of this person you've just met.

If you get together again, see if you can imagine spending more time with him or her, doing different things. Suggest one or two of them—a walk on the beach or in the woods, a play or movie, dinner and dancing—and see how she responds. Make each encounter an end in itself, not a minor scene in a much larger play—you, your life, your entire relationship history, with all the successes, failures, near misses, lost opportunities. There's plenty of time for that on other occasions.

If you learn to take love one step at a time, you'll be less prone to missteps. You'll be able to see your path more clearly and completely. You'll know what you're doing, and what each next step is. If you are truly dating the "right one," this will be as clear as anything you've ever known, but only if you go slowly, watch for all the signposts, and have in mind what you want out of this potential relationship.

D̲ay eleven   Experiment sexually. If you are at this stage of your courtship, make this a day in which you go beyond where you've been sexually in your love for each other, and express yourself in ways you haven't before. Make sure that your partner is comfortable with your intentions by discussing the broad outlines of what you would like to do before you commence, not in graphic detail but in the overall idea.

If you cannot think of things to do that you haven't done before, ask a very close friend for tips or get a suggestive book or two and read it with your partner—an activity that can be fun in itself. If you have difficulty talking about sex, write down some ideas and show them to your partner. Anything to get you and the person with whom you are intimate in the mood to feel comfortable about sexuality is what's on tap today.

Give yourself enough time to explore each other's sexuality. It probably doesn't work to have a script, but having talked about your sexual feelings or proclivities, you and your partner should have a sense of where you want to go. If the two of you are always in the same position, you might want to vary it. If the course of your lovemaking follows a predictable pattern, you might want to talk about ways of creating a different sequence of events. This might be something as basic as who initiates and who responds. Try doing it the other way. And if your initiation is verbal, try something physical. If lovemaking usually begins with someone's hand reaching out, try a well-placed whisper in your partner's ear, inviting him to do something that is not discussed in polite company.

The way to turn sex into something that enhances your intimacy is to talk about it openly and comfortably. Once you get deeply involved in your lovemaking, your plans and discussions can be put on hold and replaced by the instinctive movements of passion and desire. If your lovemaking is usually very quiet, say things. If you spend time talking a lot, try silence. If you usually make love late at night, initiate something in the morning.

Like anything else, sex benefits from attention and discussion; the recognition that what you thought you couldn't possibly do yesterday becomes tomorrow's no-big-deal. You and your partner can inspire each other to step out of your respective comfort zones and take some risks. Turn your bedroom or any other room into the laboratory in which you conduct your sensual experiments.

Intimacy and Communication for Couples

Groucho Marx once said that eighty percent of success in life is just showing up. It's the same, in a sense, with love. People who have the most successful love lives, who have love in abundance, are those who make love a priority. It's what they want, it's what guides their choices, it's what nourishes and sustains them.

Some couples coast for a time in perfect harmony. For whatever reason, either by choice or good fortune, one person's tune blends perfectly with the melody of the other. But sooner or later, most people in successful relationships have to ask for what they want. They cannot depend on telepathy for their partners to know what they need, whether it is to be closer, to have more distance, to help with the dishes, to have more sex, to spend time with the kids, to stop talking negatively about other people, to watch less sports on television, whatever it is. Successful couples know how to do this. They don't live in the fantasy world of "Well, I shouldn't have to ask him to hug me," or "She should know that it ticks me off when she works on weekends."

Love is not proud. It seeks to connect, to communicate its requirements as clearly, directly, and gently as possible. The most harmful thing in a relationship is silence—not expressing a need or feeling for fear of hurting your partner or the intimacy. It doesn't work. The world is littered with broken relationships and marriages between people who would not tell their partners what they wanted and then got angry at them for not knowing. By then it's often too late.

Couples who succeed are couples who communicate, even at the risk of momentary conflict or resentment. They understand that love is a process, not a finished product, and that ultimately it is the courage to risk equanimity for the sake of truth that drives and sustains a successful relationship.

D*ay one* Share some significant moments from your past with your partner. Be open and expansive. Make sure you include enough details about these events to make the stories interesting, to allow your significant other to understand you more deeply or in a different way.

Did you once take a backpacking trip into the wilderness alone and find that the solitude introduced you to parts of yourself you never knew existed? Did you once spend hours a day humming melodies from Bach and Mozart, which inspired you to take up the flute? Did you ever help a friend or relative through a difficult time—like the breakup of a relationship or the death of someone close —and later find it was your support or encouragement that was crucial to that person's regaining peace of mind? Tell your partner what happened. Search your memory and relive the experience as if it just took place.

Try to tell the whole story from as many points of view as possible. If you are describing how you opened up a bicycle repair shop, tell your partner what your parents thought of the idea, and how your friends reacted as well. Ask him or her to listen carefully, interrupting only to ask questions about particular details or developments of the story.

It's often a good idea to talk about your significant past relationships, to discuss how they affected you, how they changed you, what you learned from them. If you allow your partner to participate in the storytelling by asking questions and providing feedback, he or she will feel closer to you, and you will have fostered that closeness by having opened up your life in a very intimate way.

$\mathcal{D}$ay two   Spend the day with your partner—but with each of you doing your own thing. A life of intimacy does not require constant direct interaction. Being in close proximity is sometimes all that's needed to feel loved and loving.

A healthy, intimate partnership does not necessarily mean you must enjoy the same activities as your mate. Feel free to do things together if you are so inclined, but try to look at these activities as part of the natural unfolding of your relationship, rather than something that is expected or necessary. If you want to read a book while your spouse or partner makes a fruit salad, indulge in your respective pleasures. When you pass your wife on the way to the refrigerator, smile at her lovingly or kiss her on the neck and be on your way. If your partner wants to take a well-deserved afternoon nap while you clean up the house, watch television, or listen to music, that's fine, too.

What matters most in a successful intimate relationship is the feeling you have for each other, not any one way in which you relate. Some couples share many similar interests and yet don't know how to be intimate, while others with seemingly independent lives know how to make the most of their moments together and how to express their affection and regard for each other. The foundation of having a relationship that works is a sense of comfort, of security, of knowing that your partner is emotionally available even if you are not interacting directly.

If you learn how to express intimacy without being to-gether every moment, you can begin to develop a balanced relationship, one that affords you opportunities to be both alone and together in just the right measure. Couples who feel compelled to spend every spare moment doing some-thing together may at first think their togetherness is a good sign, but in time this obligatory closeness may make one or both partners feel cramped, restricted, or even suf-focated. It's better to get used to separation at the begin-ning than to face your partner's desire to create distance years later.

Day three Tell your partner what you like about him or her. It can be trivial or significant, something she does occasionally or all the time. What matters is that your husband, wife, or partner *knows* that you are seeing him or her, that you are really noticing what he or she is all about, and that you are eager to share your observations and to make your spouse aware of your loving regard and appreciation.

Your mate has an infinite number of qualities that you will find charming if you seek to notice them. Do your wife's eyes light up like two bright stars when she comes up with a good idea? Do you watch with amusement as she stands at the closet in the morning, trying to decide what to wear, her left hip thrust to the side as she places her right hand gingerly on her cheek with a look of deep concentration? Tell her about it. Explain what it's like to observe her that way, how it makes you feel, what it reminds you of, why it pleases you so much.

What about your husband? Do you find it totally endearing to watch him fixing dinner, an activity he approaches in much the same way a conductor approaches leading a symphony orchestra? Let him know. Immerse yourself in every detail and nuance, how charming the kitchen looks when each bowl, pot, and serving dish you own is used, and how he painstakingly sets the dining room table. Tell him what it does for you to see his head buried in *The Silver Palate* as if it were *War and Peace,* his concentration at its peak, his brow furrowed as he tries to decide what herbs to include or whether he should stick with the recipe or strike out on his own.

Letting your partner know what you like about him or her benefits you as well. By drawing attention to those things about your mate that please, excite, or delight you, you ensure that he will keep doing them and maybe even do them more. You are positively reinforcing things you like by expressing your delight. This works for adults and for children. People of any age are inclined to cultivate qualities that get noticed. And telling someone what you like about him or her is so much better than focusing on what you don't like.

So speak up about your partner's good qualities, even if they are qualities you've admired but never mentioned for thirty-seven years. It's not too late to compliment or commend what you find attractive about the person you've chosen to share your life with.

Day four   Create a photo album of your life to-gether. This can be done by using a video as well, editing together bits and pieces of old tapes into one grand and glorious story of you, your partner, and this wonderful, mysterious thing called your relationship.

Many couples go to great lengths and expense to put together a formal wedding album, but then ignore what follows, haphazardly keeping pictures of their times to-gether collected in boxes.

With your mate, go through your photographs and pick out your favorites, the ones that show a special time or place, that flatter you, or that have significance in any other way. Remember that each shot will have more value if there are fewer of them. You might want to add captions to your selections. Include the setting, when the shot was taken, by whom, and what circumstances prompted you to make this particular selection. Is there a photo of you during a trip to the West Coast a few months before your first child was born, or one from the days when the two of you were hippies? Include them.

This activity will also be a contemplative way to share special moments with your partner, to recall events that are significant to you, to see how far you've traveled since these photographs were taken. It will also show you how much—or how little—you've changed over the years.

Add to your album from time to time. Make it an expression of your satisfaction with your partner, and also a concrete way to rejoice in what you have built together.

Day five Enact your favorite sexual fantasy. Entice your partner to play along, to drop his or her everyday persona and become your fantasy. See if you can feel comfortable discussing what excites you, what comes to mind when you think about your ideal sexual encounter. Perhaps you've already experienced it, or maybe it exists solely in your imagination. What matters now is your ability to articulate what arouses you.

Keep in mind that your sexual fantasy may involve giving up your will to your partner. That's fine. This is an exercise in taking control of your erotic life, in directing it as if you had all the power over your partner you ever wanted. See what develops, what emerges from your mind and your emotions. Try to go beyond where you've ever sexually been before.

If the venue of this fantasy is limited to your bedroom, there's still a lot you can come up with. If you live in a warm climate and can go outside, that might get your creative juices flowing. Take a blanket and something to eat and drink, and drive to a secluded spot beside a cool pond. Hold hands walking into the woods and free your mind of everything that does not pertain to the excitement of the moment. Slowly remove each other's clothing and take a refreshing dip in the clear, inviting water.

Lie in the sun and partake of the savory delights you brought with you. Feed each other. Let your hand linger at your partner's mouth. Offer yourself to him or her. Make sure what you're doing is done with direction, that it's exactly what you or your partner has in mind. Go slowly. Take your time. Stretch out the moments so they seem to go on forever.

If you enacted your sexual fantasy, next time offer your partner the opportunity to indulge in his or hers. If you live in the middle of a big city, you may want to turn off the elevator in your apartment building, or make your way to the top floor of a grand hotel and be quick and passionate. It's your choice.

Heighten your sexual life through sharing and reciprocity, through mutual fulfillment and satisfaction.

Day six   Have an astrological compatibility chart done with your partner. You don't even have to believe in astrology to make this worthwhile. Just see it as a form of entertainment, one that can add to your understanding of what works and what doesn't in your relationship.

There's a lot more to astrology than what you see in the daily newspaper. Until about three hundred years ago, astrology was considered a science, and the movements of the heavenly bodies were thought to determine much about life here on Planet Earth.

A competent astrologer will be able to interpret both your and your partner's charts, pointing out areas in which you are compatible and others that might be in opposition. For example, although your communication may be clear and direct, you may not be giving each other enough support. Perhaps you are soul mates, but the stars may also indicate some tension if you decide to work together.

Although there are intricate aspects of your charts that will reveal more than you thought possible, the most general information concerns your Sun, Moon, and rising signs. Doing your charts together will tell you a lot about the quality of your relationship, why you are together, what you have to learn from each other, and any pitfalls you may have to watch for.

Get the stars involved in your connection. See if you can be open to guidance from a heavenly source. Even if astrology seems too far out for you, have the courage to be receptive to it anyway. Act as if you are being counseled by the universe itself.

Day seven   Share your dreams with your partner. I'm referring to your waking dreams, not your sleep dreams, although these are important, too. Your hopes and aspirations are a significant part of who you are, and divulging them to your partner will serve to create a stronger bond between you.

You can begin by talking about what you envision for yourself in your work. If you are basically happy with what you're doing, talk about that with your mate, but also tell him or her where you see yourself going over the next stretch of time. What would you like to see happen? Are you dreaming about taking your skills to the next level, where you can perform employee training and eventually learn to be a great public speaker? Talk about what that would mean to you, what it would feel like to realize this dream. If you're not happy in your work, don't withhold that, even if your partner expresses fear or concern. Have faith that sharing your dreams will guide you to do something that will satisfy and fulfill you, what Buddhists call Right Livelihood.

Now move on to other areas of life. Talk about your home or love life, the dreams you have for your children or for the world. Include as many specifics as possible, making your dreams come alive with vivid descriptions and deep feelings. Your life dreams can be large or small, grand or relatively insignificant. It doesn't matter. You could talk about your dream vacation to go on a safari, or how you see your children attending high school abroad. Or perhaps you can talk about your dream of making love on every continent, having a house with a family room where the kids can play by themselves, or living in a world where no one goes to bed hungry.

Sharing your dreams is in many ways sharing the most intimate part of yourself, the part that is leading you toward the person you are in the process of becoming. When you talk passionately about what you'd like to see happen in your life, you bring your partner into the equation. You create a relationship that is distinct from the ones you have with nearly everyone else, with co-workers and business associates, even with friends and relatives. When you share your dreams with your partner, you entrust him or her as their guardian, someone who can remind you when you are blue that you are more than what you are right now—that you are also what you imagine.

Day eight Honor the differences between you and your partner. Talk about the unique ways in which you see the world, how each of you reacts differently in certain situations, how your partnership is made stronger by acknowledging your individual but complementary skills and talents.

A strong intimate life with another person does not exclude or ignore differences. It does not pretend that two people are exactly alike, or that the parts of them that are different should be ignored so nobody is "wrong." A true partnership accepts differences. It is mature enough to recognize that no two people are the same, with identical tastes and inclinations, and that if you would rather get up at dawn, put on your sweats, and run while your partner sleeps, it doesn't make you neurotic or your partner lazy.

Both you and your relationship are large enough and strong enough to accommodate this.

Does your partner occasionally leave dirty dishes in the sink overnight, whereas you insist on cleaning the kitchen before going to bed? Talk about this. Explain to him or her how it makes you feel to see that things are not put away, but also listen to your partner's side, how he or she considers it obsessive never to break a pattern. Fashion a compromise. Make minor adjustments. Sometimes the slightest course correction can mean the difference between a relationship that endures and one that doesn't.

Day nine   Fashion a portrait of your partner. Really look at how your mate appears to you by producing a representation of him or her. There are a variety of ways to do this: you can make a drawing or painting, photograph him from a number of different angles in various settings, do a sculpture of your partner, or write a full description —either from memory or while you gaze at her.

This activity is fun, and can also lead to interesting observations about you and your partner that you never realized before. A perceived lack of artistic talent is no problem. Anyone can find a way to create a likeness, and doing so may introduce you to talents you never knew you had.

Notice the way your mate's lips meet when his mouth is closed, or how your spouse's hair falls around her ears and neck when she gets it cut. Look at your partner's hands, at the length and shape of her fingers as they taper toward her fingernails, or at his eyes as they gaze at you with a combination of awe and familiarity as you go about your work of portraying him.

Try to stimulate your partner's active participation in this process, even if his or her role is to be completely still as you work. Imagine that what you are doing is a form of making love, that it represents the very essence of intimacy that exists between you, that no one knows you better than the two of you do in this very moment.

When you are finished, show your masterpiece to your partner and discuss your work. Solicit his or her comments about the various aspects of what you've completed. Plan to have another session like this one, with the roles reversed.

Day ten   Forgive someone. It doesn't have to be your current partner, although it might be. It can be anyone—a former lover, a friend or relative, your mother or father, or a current or past business associate. Keep in mind that the person you choose to forgive is not as important as the act of forgiving.

In order to love in the present, to be fully free to love your partner, you have to clear yourself of existing barriers, and one way to do this is to forgive. Forgiveness is an act, even if it appears you're not doing anything in particular, and the person you're forgiving isn't available to hear your thoughts. The act of forgiving originates in your heart and signifies the release of a hurt that someone caused you.

Forgiveness doesn't mean you are forgetting about the person or the incident that caused you pain. You can still remember. And you may still even feel the pain. But at the same time, you consciously decide to understand that whatever this person did, he or she felt it had to be done, that the action involved lots of factors that went beyond you and your role, and that it was the only alternative this person thought was available in those circumstances.

No act is too painful not to be forgiven. If the mother of an African immigrant slain in Portland for no reason other than that he was black can publicly forgive his murderer, then you can forgive an old lover or friend for his or her transgressions, for walking out on you when you were ill, for refusing to discuss with you the demise of your relationship, or for having an affair while swearing to you it was all in your imagination. You may also choose to forgive your father for being remote and unapproachable, and for showing emotion only when you came home after curfew and broke his rules.

In fact, the very severity of the hurt makes the forgiveness all the more cleansing. You can never undo the pain you have felt, but you can begin to remove the pain in the present. Forgiving a hurt begins the process of healing and opens you up to love and intimacy right now, without the often distorted filter of the past or the potentially unrealistic expectations of the future.

$\mathcal{D}$ay eleven   Talk about money with your partner. Share your feelings about the income that keeps your
household going. Especially if you disagree about how your
funds ought to be spent or earned, it's important to talk
about your family finances. Differences of opinion about
money are the leading cause of marital discord, so you
want to preclude the possibility of such discord by airing
everything.

It's important to talk about money in depth, not just
skirt the surface. Values about money are embedded from
our childhood, and how we handle it often reflects unconscious habits learned from our parents. Are you a saver or
a spender? Do you choose to expend most of your financial
energy figuring out how to hold on to what you have or
how to bring in more? Do you worry about money? Do you
feel there's never enough? Is the accumulation of funds a
goal in and of itself for you? These and other similar questions are essential to ask yourself and your partner.

Explore the possibilities. Discuss the attitudes about
money that you feel contribute to harmony in your relationship, and those that don't. Do you need to look to the
future? Does that mean you ought to set aside some income
for retirement? Shape a way of dealing with money that
combines the best of what you know with the best of what
your partner knows. If that means making changes in the
way your household handles your funds, make them.

If you deal with money issues fully and frankly, by expressing your views and displaying the kind of behavior you think is appropriate, you will lessen the possibility of finances becoming a problem in your relationship. It's not only important to know how much you're making and what you're spending it on, it's also important to know why you're working and what you're working toward. If you can integrate finances into your overall life goals and purpose, then the question of money will be an easy one in your relationship. It will not interfere with other aspects of your intimacy that may be working well.

Day twelve Delay sexual gratification. See how long you can go without giving in to your urges—if, in fact, you have them. If you have a routine pattern of lovemaking, try to extend the periods between sexual intimacy for as long as you can. Explore other aspects of your intimate life.

Pretend you don't know about sex but are just inter-ested in being intimate. What would you do? There are ways of expressing closeness, affection, and a heightened sense of connection without sexual intercourse. What do you think they are? Consider some ways of feeling intimate with your partner without immediately getting into bed together.

What does it feel like to have a long conversation about matters so deep and so personal that you will explore them for the rest of your life? How would it feel to take a long walk, on a beach or meadow high above the hustle and bustle of everyday life, arm in arm without saying anything, wordlessly communicating as intimately as you have ever communicated? What about reading together, each of you absorbed in a wonderful story, your imaginations so engaged that you take turns reading aloud, occasionally looking over at your partner to exchange knowing glances?

If you delay sexual gratification, you give yourself the opportunity to learn other ways of developing and expressing intimacy. And when your resistance finally breaks down, when you are just bubbling over with desire, your lovemaking will be different. It will be fueled—even subconsciously—by the memories of intimate times that have occurred in the interim, and of the sensual thoughts you had during your brief period of celibacy, as you imagined yourself expressing your love for your partner in this very intimate and very physical way.

Day thirteen   Be specific when you communicate. In your interactions with your partner—be they sexual, verbal, or emotional—express yourself so that your partner understands immediately what you mean. Don't leave out important information when you are giving instructions or asking for something. Describe your wishes in precise language that leaves no doubt as to the nature and meaning of your request.

The point of all this is to avoid thinking that your

partner has ignored your request, and to avoid being angry if you believe this is true. Keep in mind that if you are specific with your partner, you are presenting him or her with a great gift, the gift of your focus and attention.

If you think of a better way for your spouse to get your eight-year-old to clean her room, suggest specific alternatives, such as "She responds better when you get down to her level and make cleanup fun. How about pretending that you're Jennifer and having her be Daddy? I'll bet she'll pick up her things really fast." Even if you think he's not doing it right, shift your thinking to what he could do right.

Think ahead. If your wife is going to make reservations for dinner at a popular restaurant, tell her before she calls to ask for a table by the fireplace, not after she's hung up the phone. If your partner has developed the habit of leaving wet towels on the bed, and you no longer want to be the one who is expected to pick them up, say so. In language that is as direct as possible, tell him that you will no longer pick up wet towels after him, and that, more important, you expect him to make a habit of hanging them up himself.

One very important thing, besides being specific and taking the time and the trouble to communicate clearly, is to state what you want and don't want in a gentle manner, one that encourages the other person to be a responsive partner. And remember that the street is two-way. Communicate constantly, and build into your relationship the freedom to ask questions and get clarification. *No one* should have to try to figure out what someone else wants.

Day fourteen   Be realistic. Let go of your idealized notion of your partner. The quicker you understand
that he or she is a real human being with imperfections
like anyone else, the sooner your relationship will be on a
sound long-term footing. Recognizing that your partner is
not perfect does not mean that you love him or her any
less, only that you recognize the impossibility of someone
else being exactly what you desire.

Get beneath the slippery surface of glossy romance and
down to the basics of intimacy. Can you speak to each
other about what is on your mind, even if it is painful or
threatening? Can you listen well to what your partner
needs from you, even if you haven't been brought up to
value listening? Can you each deal with tensions as they
occur, instead of ignoring them and hoping they will dis-
sipate? Can you break the habit of needing to get in the
last word in an argument?

When you give up the notion of the other person's perfection, in effect you are giving up the notion of your own
perfection as well. You are seeing yourself as a person who
is in a state of becoming, who is growing and learning, and
that your partner is doing the same—in his or her own
time in his or her own way. People in relationships are not
identical, and the best relationships are between people
who respect each other's paths, who act as teacher and
mentor for each other.

When you let go of an idealized notion of your partner, something else takes its place—the knowledge that your relationship is based on something genuine. It is based on a willingness to see clearly and love your partner, rather than a projection of your own mind.

Day fifteen Switch roles with your partner. For one day be the other person. If you take your kids to school every day, have your husband or wife do it today. If you cook each night and your wife cleans up, reverse the tasks and see what develops. Make sure you make a mutual pact beforehand that you can do whatever you want today the way you want to do it, that no one can compare what happens to the way things are normally done.

If you choose to take the kids to school by bus, that is your prerogative. Turning the task into an adventure might be fun—and a challenge, to boot. If you are going to cook tonight, you can make something new. Try a dish that he normally makes but in your own way, or order in from a nearby restaurant. There are no rules to follow, no patterns to adhere to. This is a day to break new ground.

What is life like for your spouse or partner? Does one of you normally answer the ringing telephone? Have the other one perform this task today. Do you object to the television being turned on immediately after dinner? Make sure you do this as well today, with the roles reversed. See what life is like from the other side.

Love thrives in an atmosphere of understanding, and one of the ways to gain this is to experience what the other person does every day, to live life as he or she lives it.

Summer

Setting the Imagination Aglow

In order to have more love in your life, first you need to imagine having it. It's that simple. If you don't imagine having it, it's not likely to happen. Very few people are "surprised" by love, in the sense of being struck by it or having it without first desiring it. And the initial act of desire comes through your imaginative powers.

Your imagination is like the wood you must use to build a fire in your fireplace. Of course you still have to open the flue, start with the kindling, make sure you have matches, keep a poker and perhaps a bellows nearby, and continually make decisions about when the fire needs to be tended, but if you don't first fuel your fire with wood, you won't get a spark going, regardless of your plans or intentions. And what's more, you have to continually toss logs in the fireplace if you want your blaze to endure.

It's the same with your imagination. Calling upon your imagination to guide your life is a deliberate act of will. Many people have difficulty using this immense power, which to me accounts for why they have very little success in their lives, however they define success. They are self-proclaimed "realists" who don't want to be Pollyannas and live "in a fantasy world." Pollyannas dream, *and do nothing but dream.* They expect love to appear in their lives without having to take action, without taking risks, without reaching out to the world around them and actively fashioning a loving life out of their experiences, attitudes, successes *and* failures, triumphs *and* tragedies. They live in a world in which they are passive observers trying to wish their love, their happiness, their success into existence.

If you want to be truly happy, or successful, and have love in your life, you have to project vivid images of the life you want. You can never neglect the reality that everything material begins somewhere in the mind/body, and is made real to you through the pictures and images you form in your mind. Your imagination is in truth what guides your life and "creates" your opportunities. There are times when the only thing you have left is your ability to dream, but with this power you are still probably ninety percent of the way toward your goal. Without it, you are still at the starting point. It is precisely your ability to maintain a clear, vivid image of having more love in your life—even, *especially,* when you appear to have none—that will constitute the foundation on which the rest of your life of love will be built.

The power to dream and envision a life filled with love is the first step to creating it materially. In fact, as soon as you imagine it, it's already yours.

$\mathcal{D}$ay one Think about something you imagined having and then received. Search your past for a time when what you dreamed about in your conscious life came to pass, whether it happened when you were a small child or last week. Whenever it was, try to reconstruct what occurred, how the idea developed in your imagination, how much you thought about it, and how it came to be.

A story from my own past will illustrate this. When I was thirteen years old I began to develop a fondness for tennis. It was largely because a classmate on whom I had a crush was taking lessons and I wanted to be able to play with her. I fantasized constantly about the two of us on the court, but I had neither a racket nor the $5 I needed to buy a beautiful wooden model I had seen in the sporting goods section of a nearby discount store. I devised all kinds of plans to try to buy this racket, but nothing worked. I never stopped thinking about it, though.

One day I was cleaning out the night table next to my bed and I found an old wallet, one I hadn't used in perhaps a year. I opened it and there, to my utter disbelief, was a five-dollar bill, folded neatly into the brown leather. Within minutes I was off to the store and became the proud owner of the racket I had imagined myself having. I played for many years with this racket and in fact did not buy a new one until sixteen years later.

I'll never forget the moment I saw the money. It was like a revelation for me, an opportunity to view myself as blessed with the good fortune to obtain what I fervently desired. I know today that what "produced" the money was my imagination. It was so important to me to have that racket that I thought about it constantly, leading me to places I might not otherwise have considered to find the money.

My imagination was the soil from which my life as a tennis player grew. And to me, it was because I had the courage to hold on to my dream of being on the court with a young girl with my own racket. In a very real sense, it was my imagination that provided the link between my budding feelings of love and my ability to act on them. This can work for you as well.

$\mathcal{D}$ay two Imagine this is your last day on earth. See if you can spend the day totally absorbed in this great transformation that is about to take place. You are not going to die, but you are in the future, about to travel to another galaxy, and you have no idea when you will return to earth. In fact, it's quite possible you won't be coming back any time soon.

Although you've heard stories, you really have no idea what life will be like when you arrive at your destination, and so you have to spend your day as if you are never going to see the same sights and hear the same sounds again. What will you do? Whom will you see? What are your last thoughts as you go about preparing to make this journey? You can leave behind anything you want. The place to which you are going will supply everything you need, so you will take only what you cherish.

How will you spend your last moments on earth? Who will you be around? What will you be doing? If you can use your imagination to see yourself at the end of your days on this planet, you can open yourself up to personal possibilities that will take you beyond where you are right now.

Imagining this is your last day on earth without thinking about the possible fright of impending death is a great way to focus on what matters, to cling to the elements of your life that are most important, that satisfy you like no others, that define and identify you.

Day three Ask someone to tell you a story. Whether he or she is seventeen or seventy-seven, think of someone you know whose storytelling abilities are of the highest order and invite him or her to your house. Prepare tea, hot chocolate, or perhaps a glass of sherry and ask a question that is sure to get him or her going. Let this person know that you've got a lot of time on your hands and that the more details he or she can supply you with, the better.

Ask questions about things you don't understand clearly. Your purpose is to hear as much as you can so that your imagination becomes truly activated. As you listen to your friend or relative tell the story, picture the events as if you were watching a movie, or as if you were with your friend when he or she first experienced these events.

Keep in mind that good storytellers can make a five-minute trip to the corner grocery store for a quart of milk and a loaf of bread sound like winning the lottery, so pick the right person. It really doesn't matter what you are about to listen to. It could be your grandmother telling you what it was like to come to America from Poland, the people she left behind, the village in which she grew up, how she met your grandfather. Or it could be a friend of yours recounting his experiences as he rode a bicycle from Vancouver to Mexico City, the people he met along the way, how many times he got rained on and what he did to protect himself, and when he felt most alone during the six-month trip. Or it could be someone inventing a story.

A good story will entice you to use your imagination. It's better than television. If you listen carefully to a friend's tale and imagine the scene, it forces you to be creative, to plumb the depths of your own past or imagination to fill in the pictures that give life and energy to the words.

$\mathcal{D}$ay four   Play the cloud game. Invite a friend or your partner to play along with you, and make sure the weather conditions are favorable for this exercise. If today turns out to be full of sunshine, wait to play this game on another occasion—one in which the sky is full of clouds.

Give yourself enough time to do this right, at least an hour. The purpose of the game is to look at the clouds and talk about the shapes they bring to mind. Clouds are just clouds, of course, but they can also be ice-cream cones, or bananas, or shaped like the state of Florida, or a horse that's galloping across a sand dune with scrubby vegetation.

What shapes do you see? A string of feathers extending from one end of the sky to the other, or a series of delicate points that make you think of Seurat's *Sunday Afternoon on the Island of La Grande Jatte?* What about at the other end of the horizon? Do you see a fluffy cloud that reminds you of the frothy top of a cup of freshly made cappuccino, which needs only a sprinkle of powdered chocolate to be completely irresistible?

What does your friend or partner see? Can you relate to his or her images, or are they completely lost on you? Can you point to some clouds and draw the outlines of the shapes that you see? How long will it take the wind to transform your ocean liner into a picket fence that rings a large grassy area?

If you play the cloud game, you are using your imagination to guide you through the maze of shapes that continually confront you. See if you and your companion can get wild and identify the Tower of London or a fancy evening dress or a palm tree with most of its branches removed. See if you can massage your imagination to see people, faces, downy comforters, intricate postage stamps, or the faces on Mount Rushmore. Ask your imagination for guidance. Tell it that it has no limits, that it can see whatever it wants to see.

Day five Begin reading a great novel. It can be something you've read before and enjoyed, or a book that has been recommended to you by someone whose opinion you value. What's important is that you embark on a journey that takes you into a world created by the author's imagination, and that you use your imagination to make that world come alive.

It doesn't matter that you didn't live in the nineteenth century and that you've never been to England. The novels of George Eliot or Thomas Hardy will provide you with every opportunity to live the life and feel the feelings of nineteenth-century English characters. Do you want to know what it was like to live in the twenties? Read the works of F. Scott Fitzgerald or Ernest Hemingway, which take place in that decade.

Did you ever notice that even if a movie version of a novel is great, it's never as satisfying as the novel itself? Why? Perhaps it's because reading a good book opens you to the world of your imagination; you can linger over a word or a passage for as long as you want, you can fill in the blanks, and you can supply the images to go with the words the author provides. How can it be that great writing moves you, makes you feel something deeply, stays with you long after you've forgotten the words? I still vividly

infinite reservoir of power that supplies you constantly with what you require to remain healthy.

Now imagine doing whatever it takes to remain in this state. If that means eating right, then see yourself choosing whole foods that are low in fat, salt, sugar, and preservatives. If being healthy means exercising more, then picture yourself in motion, your heart rate up, perspiring slightly, doing whatever it takes to stay fit and feel good at the same time.

Just keep a picture in mind of your body looking and feeling exactly the way you want it to, and that you are loving and accepting it as it is. Imagine also that what's going on deep inside your being reflects what's happening on the surface. At a certain point, your inner and outer lives will merge and become one. Your outer beauty will blossom as you become healthier and more self-accepting. And the better your body feels and looks, the more beautiful you become on the inside.

A life filled with love includes and incorporates the physical, with a body that is capable of loving and being loved because it is filled with energy and has the drive to attract that which is healthy, nurturing, and full of vitality.

Day eight Imagine yourself as part of a loving, supportive family. Regardless of the way you currently feel about your family, even if you come from and are still part of one that is dysfunctional, see each member in harmonious balance with you and with every other individual in your family, whether he or she is your mother, father, sister, or brother, a member of your extended family, or a member of your wife's family. Focus on what your family could be, how you would in fact like to see it.

See if you can picture yourself at a large gathering, perhaps a wedding, a reunion, or a birthday celebration. Visualize all your close relatives being there, partaking of the merriment, each enjoying himself or herself in precisely the manner he or she wishes. Some will be dancing, others talking animatedly, still others quietly and contentedly taking in the festivities.

Imagine yourself connecting with everyone at the gathering, that you are able to feel love for each of your family members, and that you are able also to feel their love for you. A word, a glance, a smile, an embrace may be all you need to acknowledge the bond that exists between you. With some people, you may want to engage more fully, to reminisce about the time your cousin first took you ice skating, or when you and your sister baked an angel-food cake for Mother's Day. You may also want to demonstrate your love for your uncle by listening to the details of his life with your aunt, who passed on many years before.

What's important here is not the venue or the particular circumstances. What matters is the effort to imagine your family life as balanced and loving, with disputes and other conflicts resolved quickly and with satisfaction all around; you may feel yourself supporting and being supported by the rest of your family, and everyone is demonstrating in his own way regard for the family as a whole and for each individual member.

The first step to being part of such a family is to imagine this scenario clearly. Visualizing a harmonious family on which you can count and in which you participate fully creates a powerful message that in time will be manifested. How this comes to be may be completely different from how you imagine it happening, but you'll recognize the feeling.

The task is never to try to "change" family members or to encourage them to behave differently, but always to imagine everyone feeling so fulfilled and confident that no one ever wants to control anyone else.

Day nine   Picture your life as blessed with many good friends. See yourself as part of a network of people who make time to speak with or see one another—frequently or occasionally. What's important is the quality and depth of the interactions.

Picture you and your friends laughing and talking together, sharing the ups and downs of your lives, discussing matters that are important, amusing, or perplexing. Envision yourself valuing the presence in your life of someone who is special to you, whose counsel you esteem, who delights in what delights you, who supplies a perspective that you can't get from members of your family because they

may be too close to you and too enmeshed in your particular situation to provide wise and consistent counsel.

Imagine that you build your friendships for life, that
regardless of the frequency of contact, you keep friends in
your orbit. See yourself picking up where you left off, con-
versing whenever you encounter your friend as if no time
had passed, even if years have gone by.

Picture your life enriched over the years by your friendships, how you celebrate your lives together. Imagine that
you accommodate, accept, or tolerate the myriad changes
that take place over the years, that you come through for
your friends when they need you, that they make you feel
special, that they participate in the important moments of
your life.

See if you can imagine your friendships as a microcosm
of the love that exists throughout your life and in the
world, of the reciprocity and mutual regard with which
your life is saturated. See if you can allow yourself to regard the overall condition of your life by the quality—and
not the quantity—of your friendships.

Day ten   Visualize yourself as part of a community, of a wide assortment of people who share common
values, joys, and priorities. The members of this community
do not have to live geographically close to you, although
in the traditional sense of the term this is what community
has always looked like. With the advent of modern times,

however, with people constantly moving, with communities being formed of divergent cultures, it might make sense to look for your community among people who share some common heritage, be it ethnic, religious, political, cultural, or social. Or you might want to cut right through the apparent differences with your neighbors and build a community by organizing block parties with the families that live in close proximity to you.

The point is to imagine yourself connected to a greater whole; imagine that your life takes on meaning because you are able to share the way you look at things with people who understand your goals and aspirations. You could form a community around your child's school, a sport you enjoy playing, or a political cause you hold in especially high regard. Picture yourself enriching your community with your loving attention, with the kind of care and concern you reserve for the matters most dear to you.

Envision your community growing and developing, its purpose deepening and becoming more real. Picture the interaction of people and ideas giving you the opportunity to learn more about yourself and your world through the experience of others. See your community adapting as new people enter it, as emerging leaders and spokespeople share their vision of the community's purpose, sending the group off in new, unexplored, yet potentially exciting directions.

Imagine your community making a difference in your life, in the lives of its members, and then in the wider world. See the association gently and carefully providing insight for those who may or may not agree with its purpose or point of view. See yourself as an embodiment of its ideals, of its mission, even if it's not one that is important enough to ultimately affect the course of history. Whatever the community's purpose, its significance lies in the strength of the allegiance of its members.

Day eleven   At various moments—waiting on line to see a movie, before falling asleep, while sharpening your pencil—in your mind's eye immerse yourself in play, in activities with no purpose other than your rest, relaxation, entertainment, or diversion. See yourself fully engaged in whatever it is that appeals, delights, or excites you; see yourself involved completely and actively, with no guilt or hesitation.

Visualize yourself traveling to a place that is set up solely for your enjoyment. Imagine that the trip itself is pleasurable, a perfect start to what will become a prolonged experience of playful activity, or calm, centered rest. You can envision this place anytime the mood strikes you. The place can change from time to time, or remain the same. What you do when you arrive is also up to you. The people who accompany and play with you are likewise yours to choose, as is the length of time they spend with you.

Once you arrive at your destination, follow your desires and inclinations. If your idea of play is to lie in a hammock between two palm trees on a beach in Tahiti, reading your favorite magazines while you sip a refreshing tropical drink, then imagine yourself right there. Perhaps your idea of fun is a vigorous game of volleyball at a local park on a bright Sunday morning, surrounded by strong, sleek, semi-naked men. If it is, then by all means indulge yourself.

See yourself as a soul who knows how to play, who can delight in the possibilities that each moment offers you. Imagine that you were placed on this earth as a playful being, that your life is devoted to finding out what captivates you, what makes you so glad to be alive that you constantly feel like shouting from the roof or mountaintops. Reflect back to the time when you were a child and summer vacation seemed like an eternity, as one day spilled playfully into the next and you thought summer would never end. See if you can recreate that feeling as you imagine your playful side activated and engaged, involved in pursuits that make time less important.

Allow your entire body to relax, your breathing to deepen, and your "shoulds" to dissolve as your imagination places you in pleasurable situations or circumstances; and allow yourself to feel deserving of this possibility, all too often neglected, that life offers us.

Day twelve   Imagine yourself doing your true life's work. Do you manage stock portfolios but really want to be a professional photographer? See yourself in the

darkroom, developing prints of city scenes, interesting people, or exotic countries. Imagine what your day as a photographer would be like, when you would shoot, how you
would prepare, with whom you would discuss your work,
how you would choose your equipment, what it would *feel*
like to get up in the morning knowing your day was devoted
to taking pictures.

See yourself as a successful person, however you define
success. That may be in monetary terms, but it certainly
doesn't have to be. You may want to be a great teacher or
musician, or take part in an important new discovery that
prolongs and enhances life. See yourself in possession of
the qualities that define and enable success—great vision,
persistence, support, receptivity—so that your success and
well-being are merely the logical result of the characteristics you bring to everything you do and touch.

Imagine that your life is an opportunity to find out who
you are, and that you can and must change your values,
attitudes, and behavior as you mature and grow wise. Now
also imagine that your creativity and your self-expression
are indissolubly linked, that you are living and working in
a world in which your talents, skills, and abilities reflect
the depth of your passion and feeling about life. See your
achievements as a natural outgrowth of who you are and
who you aspire to be, and see that your work, your material
well-being, and your success are all integrated to reflect
your personal evolution at any given point in your life.

Years ago, when I thought I was stuck in a corporate
position that did not suit me, I wrote down a description
of myself that reflected the person I wanted to be. My

description included my home, my job, the ways in which I spent my days, and the people I spent them with. I spent my lunch hours walking around the neighborhood, endlessly repeating my professional "mantra." Within months I had left that job, and my life today is remarkably close to what I then imagined it to be.

Day thirteen If you are unattached, imagine that your partner is here with you, that he or she has come into your life and has brought the opportunity for you to feel your deepest feelings, share your innermost thoughts, believe in your most ardent aspirations. See the two of you sharing quiet moments together, allowing your personalities to emerge as you let go of judgment and defenses. Learn to trust the wisdom of the moment, to know that what wants to come forth is stronger and truer than anything you can devise or create.

Allow your imagination to see yourself meeting your true partner. Perhaps he is at a party at which you've just arrived, and although there are lots of people somehow he manages to get over to you. Or you are introduced by the host. You shake hands and begin to converse and before long you sense that this is a person of quality, that he has integrity and depth, and that it might be possible for the two of you to appreciate each other's gifts.

Now imagine yourself spending time on a first date. You take in a movie, but really you can't wait for the show to end because all you want to do is talk with him, to find out more about him, where he's been, what he's seen, the breadth of his experiences. You go to a place nearby and order coffee and somehow find yourself talking as if you've known this person all your life. You also talk about your life, and much to your astonishment and pleasure, he is just as interested in you as you are in him.

He promises to call you to go on a hike and in a few days, he does. You get together again, and whatever feelings of awkwardness or discomfort you may have anticipated vanish immediately. You pick up the thread of your last conversation as if it had never ended. You feel as if you want to pinch your arm to make sure all this is real.

Now see the relationship deepening, the trust building, the exploration of common ground expanding. See yourself able to navigate the inevitable rough waters together and emerge intact, the two of you more understanding toward each other than you were before.

Make up your own scenario. If you can do this, if you can actually see the beginning and development of an intimate relationship, you bring it that much closer. Although the actual relationship may not happen as you imagine it, your willingness to have faith in its certainty contributes to its eventual appearance in your life.

Day fourteen   Act as if your life is immersed in intimacy, as if your days are replete with romantic love, physical closeness, and sensuality, and as if you are draw-ing to you the people, places, and things to which you are attracted. Imagine that you are in sync with your partner, that the two of you communicate in a way that goes beyond words, that you understand each other fully, that your love is mature and developed, and that you do not have to live in a fantasy world where everything is perfect in order to feel loved and accepted.

If you are part of a couple, see yourself lifting the intimacy you share with your partner to new heights, mak-ing the effort to learn more about him or her, to find out how you can be more supportive. Envision that you can feel your love on a palpable, sensuous level, that you see your lover as if for the first time and are as dazzled by his or her charms as you were when you first met.

In your mind's eye, explore the world of intimacy together—the physical, the emotional, the spiritual, and the mental connections. See if you can keep your relation-ship fresh, constantly adding new twists and elements to it as you both grow as individuals. Also, see yourself taking care to nurture what you have created—the relationship that you formed and that you continue to hold dear. See if you can imagine yourself as a sensitive lover, a best friend, a constant source of aid and comfort.

Also see yourself in possession of the rewards of this effort and intention—of love and kindness and gener-osity that permeate your entire life and the lives of those around you.

Day fifteen   Imagine yourself in perfect harmony with the world you don't see—the Invisible World,
the world that pulsates outside the range of human certainty but nevertheless exists as surely as you and I, without our knowing much about it.

This is the world of Faith, of the Sacred, the Divine,
the world of Spirit and Energy that inhabits every one of
the billions of cells in your body and is also so vast as to
make whatever you can conceive about the universe seem
small. This is the world that cannot be named or defined
because it can never be known except in the most limited
way. This is the Invisible World. Now imagine yourself a
vital part of all this, of that which cannot be seen. Imagine
that your very existence is dependent on this world, that
it gives both life and meaning not only to you but to everything around you, and that it can manifest itself in any
form it wishes because it is inherent in everything that
exists.

Consider the other names for this world—God, the
Almighty, Christ, the One, the Tao (Way), the Unconscious,
the Universe—and choose one with which you are most
comfortable. Your name for this presence is relatively unimportant. It's all you can conceive and more. It's the life
force that enables my fingers at this very moment to move
rapidly across this keyboard, expressing the thoughts I
wish to communicate to you, and also what enables you to
read and absorb my words and sentences.

Now imagine that your relationship to this entity is the most important relationship of your life, that how you live relative to the unknowable and the unknown determines everything else that goes on in your world—both the ups and the downs, the successes and failures, the tragic and the triumphant. See your life as a long, protracted, heroic effort to get closer to the Invisible, to aspire to be worthy of having bits and pieces of the Invisible revealed to you —only to know, at the same time, that the effort is ultimately futile, that you can never fully comprehend the Invisible World because if you did, it wouldn't be invisible. See if you can understand that this world will reveal itself to you in startlingly unexpected ways over time, when it determines that you are ready to receive it.

Imagine that in the final analysis your ability to have love in your life is dependent on this one relationship, on the way in which you treat that which you cannot see, cannot know, and cannot understand. Since love is often a journey into the unknown, and is also resistant to "control" or manipulation, your ability to form a nourishing relationship with the Invisible World is the crucible in which your success in love—in its many glorious forms— will be formed.

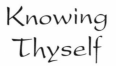

Knowing Thyself

People who derive the most pleasure from their relationships with others derive pleasure from their relationships with themselves. They realize that, fundamentally, their own lives are laboratories in which they practice how to love.

Once you learn this principle, it becomes much easier to develop loving relationships with others, because you have experience developing a loving relationship with yourself. You practice the skill of constantly checking in with your moods and emotions, and if you know what to do to make yourself feel better, and act upon this information, you begin to learn how to enter into a relationship with another and have the most fulfilling relationship possible.

There is a fine line, however, between loving yourself enough and thinking about yourself too much, essentially to the exclusion of others. I meet and work with many people who live and operate too far from the line—on both sides. On the one hand, many people are primarily concerned with the quality of their own lives. They are masters at figuring out what they want, need, like, and dislike, but have no idea how to incorporate the requirements of others into their personal equation. On the other hand, some people live their lives forever trying to calculate what everyone else wants. When you ask them what they want, what would make them happy, they may not be able to answer right away, and their response is usually about something external to themselves.

The way I see it, both types of people don't like or love themselves enough. They lack what is commonly called self-esteem. They have difficulty meeting their own needs and either focus on them obsessively—to the exclusion of the needs of others—or have given up altogether trying to get their needs met and no longer have any idea what they are. Both types of people have difficulty loving healthily. The first type has trouble forming bonds at all, or making and keeping commitments, and generally cannot integrate his life with the lives of others. The second type loves obsessively, looks to relationships with other people to make him happy, and generally focuses too much on his connection with others and not nearly enough on what is going on inside himself.

A healthy self-relationship is balanced. It is neither excessively self-involved nor not involved enough. Your needs are important, but so are the needs of others. You take time for yourself—and you make time for the people who form your life's network. Keep in mind, however, that this balance is dynamic. It is always necessary to make sure that what was in balance yesterday is still in balance today. So you must develop the means to check in with yourself, to listen and be open to the input of others, and to be courageous enough to make changes when necessary. Making time for yourself one day can turn into neglecting the needs of others who are close to you another. And letting more people into your emotional orbit can cause you to lose sight temporarily of what you require.

In the end, the old saying is true: "You can't love anyone else if you don't love yourself." The quality of the love you create in your own life, *for your own life,* will be reflected in every one of your other relationships, whether it's with your spouse or partner, your sister, or your boss. If you're having difficulty with some people, if there are problems with others that you cannot seem to figure out or resolve, look inside, at how you feel about yourself. That's where you will find both the source of the problem and the resolution, in the way in which you relate to that particular quality or characteristic in yourself. When you accept yourself—the aspects of yourself that you admire and the aspects you don't—you can then accept and love others.

$\mathcal{D}ay$ one Spend time alone. Get to know yourself—your moods, your habits, your thoughts, the content and quality of your inner life. If you can manage to spend the entire day by yourself, with no distractions, creating your own schedule, doing as you please, it will help you to get reacquainted with the person you are, rather than the person everyone expects you to be.

Go to the beach and sit by the ocean, listening to the waves as they crash against the sand or rocks. Visit a museum and gaze at your favorite paintings or sculptures. What do you think of them? Are they what you consider art to be? Try to develop your own sense of what art is. Or you can spend the day without plans, letting the meandering course of the moment carry you along. See if time moves more slowly or more quickly than you imagined it would.

One of the keys to a loving life is to love your own life, to take in what's around you through your own filter, unencumbered by the judgments and interpretations of others.

If you already spend a lot of time by yourself, if indeed you sometimes feel you are alone too much, see if you can make the time productive by devoting your energy toward a creative project—like artwork, writing, or playing a musical instrument.

If you must make special arrangements to carry out this suggestion, begin now. Ask people around you to give you the gift of some time alone. You'll be able to love more fully and directly when you know what it is you love, and you'll be able to understand this better when you can immerse yourself in solitude.

Day two   Make a list of your accomplishments. Sit down with a pad of paper or your favorite notebook and start thinking about what you have achieved in your life. Your list can include big things or little ones, everything from putting yourself through graduate school, to spending six weeks in South America alone, to giving your turtle a decent burial when you were a youngster.

Try to remember particular things. Did you give up smoking twelve years ago? Record all the feelings associated with this achievement. Talk about your fears, what it was like to see other people light up after you had quit. Discuss the physical sensations, and the feeling when you realized you were going to succeed.

Perhaps you aced a math final in your junior year of high school after getting Cs and Ds throughout the semester. How did you pull this off? What motivated you to want to succeed, and what steps did you take to act on your intention? Did you finally go to a tutor? Did she explain the principles of trigonometry in a way your regular teacher never had? What did it feel like to catch on? Were you confident or fearful going into the exam? Write it all down.

List as many things as you can think of. Talk to people who know you and were there with you at crucial times, and ask them to fill in whatever blanks exist. Add to your list when something pops into your head. The longer your list, the more clearly you'll see how able, remarkable, and unique you are, how much and how well you have lived—and loved.

Day three   Straighten your posture. See yourself as a majestic redwood—tall, erect, perpendicular to the earth, reaching up to the heavens with a combination of passion and ease—that also must be firmly rooted in Mother Earth in order to have such a reach.

Imagine you are a puppet, with a string that is attached to your spine and that goes up your back and out of the top of your head, and that the heavens are gently pulling on this string to make your body properly aligned. Whenever you feel yourself slouching, remember the string and you'll straighten up.

See if you can place your weight evenly between your front and back—not too far in either direction. If your weight is ahead of you, it might mean you are too aggressive and can therefore be knocked off balance—figuratively speaking—from the rear. If your weight is behind you, it probably means you are too passive and can be intimidated by what's ahead. If you can move your weight to the center, you'll create balance and harmony, and you'll find your capacity to love will increase because you'll always be where you should be.

Holding yourself upright is a sign that you are not weighted down by the pressures and tensions of everyday living, that you see clearly and with an even perspective, and that you can receive the gifts of others and of the universe openly and with grace. Remember the redwood tree, firmly rooted, erect, and reaching up as high as it can go. See if you can embody the ancient wisdom of "As above, so below."

$\mathcal{D}$ay four   Pay attention to your responses, the way you react moment by moment. Are you happy or sad? Do you get angry or tense at provocations? Or are you relaxed and enjoying yourself most of the time? See if you can spend the day being aware of how you interact with your environment, how you feel when someone says something that you either like or don't like, and what you think about when you see or hear something that triggers a response in you.

Observe yourself as you go about your daily routines—playing with your children, driving your car to work, observing an encounter between two strangers, or chatting with a friend. See what it feels like to be you. Are you content to be where, what, and who you are? Or are you elsewhere, distracted by thoughts of other times, other things, other people in other situations?

Try to experience this activity without judgment, without deciding that you are either a good or bad person for the things you say, feel, or think. Just take note of your reactions—how you stand when your boss tells you what he or she wants to have done, or whether you listen fully to your teenager when she tries to explain to you how difficult it is to make friends with the kids she admires at school.

The first step to developing a loving relationship with yourself, or to changing anything about your life, if that's your desire, is to look at what you're like, to understand how you respond to things in your life. The more openly and honestly you can do this, the easier it is to make these changes.

Day five   Accept your body. Look at it as it is, and even if you're not crazy about its size or shape, accept it anyway. Don't be intimidated or ashamed because you don't look like the men and women you see in magazines, on billboards, in movies, or on television. Most people just don't look like that, and measuring yourself against that standard will only make you miserable.

Tell yourself that no one else in the world looks like you. Keep in mind that you can always want to be an inch taller or five pounds lighter, or have fuller lips, smaller ears, thicker hair, slimmer hips, or a flatter stomach. And chances are with plastic surgery or a lot of work you could do any of these things. But what's the point? You either like the way you look or you don't, and all the changes you can imagine will not substitute for a positive body image.

When I was in my early twenties I had a huge, robust, full head of hair, but I had always wished I were taller (I'm 5'6"). I was once introduced to a man who was about 6'2" and wearing a hat. We talked, and after a while I mentioned that if I had one wish I would want to be taller. He promptly removed his hat, revealing a shiny bald dome, and said to me, "And I wish I had your hair."

Everybody has something that someone else wants. The point is not to envy others but to accept yourself as you are. You may want to accentuate what you like about yourself and live with what you don't, and if you truly accept yourself, before long none of it will matter. You'll see yourself the way others see you—charming, lovable, bright, interesting—and whatever warts you have will become part of your individual "perfection."

Day six Let go of limitations. Stop thinking that you can't do something, that it's not "practical" or "realistic," that things can never be perfect, that you can't have everything. If the only reason you think these things is that you've never experienced the other side, turn the equation around and consider the possibility that they've never happened because you never thought they could.

One of my favorite children's stories (I have two small boys) is *The Little Engine That Could.* It captures so sweetly the idea that you can do what you think you can. In the story, no one believes that the little engine can pull the broken-down train over the mountain to bring food and toys to the children who live in the valley on the other side. But the little engine starts off and keeps saying, "I think I can, I think I can, I think I can." Finally, it's clear the engine is going to succeed, and this of course drives him on, and when he arrives in the valley a hero, to cheers and accolades, he responds by saying, "I thought I could, I thought I could, I thought I could."

Limitations originate in your mind; that's where they take root and grow. Soon they are as much a part of your personal landscape as anything else, and in time you begin to act in accordance with these limiting beliefs. They can take any form, from believing you can't meet someone who will love you, to believing you can't have a career that will satisfy both your financial and emotional needs, to believing you can't have a mutually respectful relationship with your father, to believing you can't beat your brother-in-law on the tennis court. If that's what you think, that's what will be.

If you learn to let go of limiting beliefs, life at once becomes your own creation and you really begin to live realistically. If you consider yourself the master of your own fate, if you understand the connection between what you think and what materializes in time, you'll see that you can basically have whatever you want and that your task is really to figure out what that is. Be the little engine that could. Start by saying, "I think I can, I think I can."

$\mathcal{D}$ay seven Pay no attention to what others think of you. For one day, have no regard for the opinions of other people. Act as if you never learned to consider the opinions of others as having any consequence in your life. Instead, be guided by your own inner voice, the melody of your own solitary song.

Be resolute about this. If you regularly discuss your ideas and plans with people who are close to you, you can politely listen to their opinions and advice, but be impervious to them today. If you want to get your hair cut simply because you feel you need a change in your life, try to block out the words of caution from your friends. You may have beautiful hair that is the envy of everyone in your circle, but if you want to cut it, feel free. If you don't like the new you, don't worry, your hair will grow back.

Be especially leery of people who give advice based on their own experience, assuming it's the same as yours. Everyone's experience is different, and what works for one person doesn't necessarily work for another. Learn to filter out what other people say. Sometimes other people have their own agenda, and it might cloud their advice. If you are thinking of leaving your job to devote all your time to writing, or starting your own business, put the naysayers in proper perspective. There will always be people who tell you that your ideas will not work out, that you'll go broke, that you'll suffer, or that you'll regret your decision.

Developing a loving and healthy sense of self means

learning how to take the advice—often unsolicited—of others and integrate it with your own inner voice. Depending too heavily on the opinions of others will tempt you to question your own motives too much and too often. Even if other people's opinions turn out to be right, even if your venture does not succeed as you might have hoped, your boldness is nevertheless rewarded with wisdom, experience, and the understanding that you can act on your own ideas without waiting for the permission of others.

Day eight Enjoy what you eat but don't get full. Eat only enough to satisfy yourself, but stop before you think you've had enough. See what you feel like in twenty minutes or so. Eat mindfully, focusing on every mouthful, being conscious of what you are doing, how you are eating, the feelings you are having as you ingest your body's fuel. Enjoy the pleasure of the various tastes and textures.

A loving life is a life of feelings, of knowing what's going on inside you—mostly in your heart, but also in your mind and body. Many people use food to repress what's going on internally, to prevent themselves from experiencing their emotions fully. One way to become aware of how you use food is to eat enough to feel satisfied but not get full, to stop short of becoming emotionally dulled, and instead become aware of everything you're feeling, whether it is boredom, anxiety, loneliness, or joy.

For one day, pay attention to yourself by paying strict

attention to what you eat. Learn to see eating not only as a way of satisfying your physical requirements and providing yourself with a series of pleasurable experiences, but also as a way of checking in with your emotional life.

$\mathcal{D}$ay nine Simplify your life. Practice the philosophy of Thoreau when he lived blissfully by Walden Pond: "Simplify, simplify, simplify."

To make your life simple you first must get rid of everything you don't need, everything that doesn't work or isn't contributing to the possibility of having more love. I don't suggest you do this irresponsibly, but rather that you go through the balance sheet of your life and see what's expendable, what's costing you a lot, either financially or emotionally. Do you spend too much time gossiping? Have you committed yourself to people, classes, and activities that require you to be out most evenings? Do you have trouble saying no to people who want some of your time? Spend today thinking about how much of this you can eliminate.

You don't have to go through your life with a meat cleaver and get rid of your teenaged daughter, your job, your mortgage, your second car, and your sister-in-law. You only need to start considering what you could do without. Some things, like old clothes you no longer wear, are relatively easy to give away and don't require a change in your lifestyle. Other things—the development of your career, certain relationships that aren't working, where you live, how much time you spend getting to work—may be more complicated, may require more effort before switching gears. Simplifying your life may take months or even years to accomplish. But you have to start sometime, and today's the day.

$\mathcal{D}$ay ten   Develop a moral compass. Begin to put together a personal philosophy, a way of life that works for you—how to act, how to relate to others and yourself, what you consider right and wrong, who and what to be kind to, and when. You may already have developed something like this but may never have thought about it so carefully. That's fine. Spend some time thinking about your ideas. You may want to write them down on a sheet of paper or record them on an audiotape. Perhaps there is someone in your life—a good friend or relative—to whom you can write all this in a letter. Or maybe you'd want to call someone and get together with him or her to discuss these ideas, because you think more clearly when you can bounce ideas off someone else. Whatever method you choose, begin to see who you are by what your personal morality is.

You can also call these principles your ethics. Do you live by the Golden Rule? Do you draw your moral or ethical sustenance from religious teaching, or are you more secular, tending to see things from a scientific or humanistic standpoint? Are you able to act in accordance with your values, especially when you are tested? Do you believe in the importance of this world, this lifetime, or are you waiting for a better life in some other time and place?

A moral or ethical compass is useful not only for day-to-day matters but for times when things are not going as well as you would like them to. It is these special or extraordinary times when you may be forced to draw on the reservoirs of faith that materialize only when you have a deep and abiding sense of yourself—of your strengths and weaknesses, your abilities and limitations, what really matters to you, and what can easily be left behind.

Ask the people close to you for input. See if you can learn something from them about how you might choose to live your life, and then begin to make any changes in your own values that seem necessary. Remember, your moral compass is not absolute. It evolves as you live and learn. Keep in mind my favorite professor's oft-quoted phrase from Emerson: "A foolish consistency is the hobgoblin of little minds."

Day eleven Think about someone you respect deeply. It can be anyone—a friend or relative with a remarkable skill; a public figure, either living or dead, whose achievements were so great that they broadened your sense of what human beings can accomplish; or perhaps an entertainer or sports figure who has stretched his or her talent almost beyond your comprehension.

How does it make you feel when you ponder this person's achievements? Are you at all envious of his abilities, fame, or fortune? What makes him deserve the accolades that you or society has bestowed on him? If this person is close to you, can you tell him how awestruck you are by him, how much you admire and respect what he has accomplished? Get together and talk about it. See what this person says. How does he handle your praise? What is his reaction? Is it surprise? Or does he absorb your admiration easily, with nonchalance and grace?

When you think of someone you respect, you deepen the process of self-understanding by focusing on those qualities in someone else that appeal to you. If you find out more about this person, you may discover you are perfectly capable of exhibiting these qualities yourself, of being someone others respect. The line between great success and ordinary existence is very thin, and someone you admire may provide some information about greatness that will help you learn something new about yourself.

Day twelve   Take your time. Regardless of what you are doing, slow down today. Throw away the notion that the more you get done the better you are, and instead work steadily but slowly at whatever you undertake, lovingly applying yourself to the task or series of tasks you choose to perform.

Pretend you are living in another era, when the pace was slower and much less was expected of people. Imagine what life was like before the advent of tight deadlines, modems, fax machines, and overnight mail, when people prided themselves not on how fast they could perform but on how well; a time when careful attention to every detail was never sacrificed to speed and the ethic of the assembly line, a time when time was not money. Think of the Middle Ages, when a craftsman would take weeks or even months to make a barrel or a wooden eating bowl, or a shoemaker a pair of shoes.

Don't hurry today. Whether this is a regular workday and you are at the office, on the shop floor, or at the store, or you are at home with your children, or spending the time alone, slow down and try to experience your life as well as live it, without exclusively thinking about what you have to accomplish. Find out why *domani,* tomorrow, is such an important word in Italian culture by adopting the pace that gives rise to the concept. Remember, people from long ago knew the value of this way of living when they came up with the aphorism "Haste makes waste."

If you make a habit of slowing down your life's pace and taking off the pressure you have placed on yourself, lots of other changes will occur in your life. You will be more patient, more tolerant, more understanding. You will accept only those assignments that feel right to you, and you will also be in sync with love's pace, which is mindful and deliberate.

Day thirteen Laugh about a setback. This is perhaps the most difficult thing for some of us to do, to rear back and let go a tremendous peal of laughter when something happens to us that we didn't foresee or welcome. But sometimes it is the most appropriate response possible.

Laughing in the face of heartache or loss, at the sudden and complete realization that we have been fooled once again by life, that just when we were certain something was definitely going our way, our very capable opponent, life, came up with a move that threw our plans totally up in the air—laughing is sometimes the only countermove that succeeds in this game.

It doesn't matter in which area of life this temporary defeat occurs—whether in business, work, love, family, friendship—sometimes the best response is to laugh at it, at the folly of thinking the situation would turn out one way when it so obviously turned out another, at thinking you knew when you didn't know, at forgetting that we are not in control of every detail of our lives.

You may not be able to laugh exactly when you want to. It may be professionally inappropriate to laugh when you find out a big account you were working on went to another company and your boss stands before you ashen-faced. Or you may be reprimanded by your spouse for laughing if the bank turns down your application for a car loan. If that's the case, you can laugh inwardly as you play the role of a serious person, putting on your most grim countenance and using your deeply furrowed brow to indicate your profound concern. You can laugh out loud later, when no one can keep you from reacting to the absurdity of life as we live it today, a life of waiting and wanting.

Go ahead, try it. The next time you are dealing with an important matter over the phone, are transferred to three different people, finally get to someone who will help you, and then lose the connection, calmly put down the phone and laugh like a hyena.

Day fourteen Celebrate the ordinary. See the specialness in the little things that would normally go by unnoticed, the way the light from the summer sun strikes the window of a tall building downtown, setting off a reflection that turns the whole street into an orange glow. Maybe you can take special note of your kids today. I love it when my two-year-old wants a lot of something and says, "Whole bag, whole bag."

There is an infinite number of moments like this every day, and if you want to have more love in your life, a sure way to help make it happen is to notice as many of these moments as you can. When you wake up today, look over at your husband and see how his ear peeks out from the covers even though his entire body seems to be buried in the bed.

At work, take note of the way the person who delivers

your interoffice mail nods swiftly and decisively as you thank him for his efficiency, or of the pictures the man in the deli draws on your bag. On your way home, notice how your dry cleaner counts out your change from the twenty-dollar bill you gave her, patiently identifying every nickel and dime until all the money that's coming to you is in your hand.

You don't have to make a big deal about moments like these, you only have to observe them, to honor them with your momentary attention, to give thanks or say a one-second prayer of gratefulness that life is offering you the opportunity to experience and enjoy these tidbits. All you have to do in return is have the humility to acknowledge the gift.

The only difference between the ordinary and the extraordinary is your perception. If you find yourself constantly disappointed by life, in a perpetual state of irritation and frustration, if people and situations don't measure up to your standards, start looking at life one moment at a time. See the value, the beauty, and the love that exist whenever you stop what you are doing and tell yourself that each moment is a hologram—that all you ever need to know about love, all the love that exists and will ever exist, is present right here and right now.

Day fifteen   Sit calmly. Find the time to be by yourself in a quiet place without distraction. If you do this early in the morning or late at night, you may find these the most quiet times, but even if you can't spend time alone then, do it whenever you can. You may have to go to a library, church, or temple to get away from the racket of the normal day, but these places are available to you. My wife and I found the cathedral in Siena, Italy, to be a superb place to sit quietly and just be alone with our thoughts during our week there, and we managed to find time each day to visit this spot, collect ourselves, and slow down our pace. But of course anywhere will do.

When you sit quietly, be sure you are comfortable. Uncross your legs and arms and see if you can shut off your mind by letting each thought pass through without comment or judgment, almost as if the thought were being produced by someone else. For the first few minutes your mind might race, but after a while it will slow down and realize that you want it to be still and not disturb you.

Remember, you have no goal other than to spend time with yourself doing nothing, with no movement, calculation, or purpose. You are not trying to do anything—either to meditate or relax or get in touch with your higher self or reach any kind of state of Nirvana. You are only trying to be still, to shut off every part of you that is stimulated or requires stimulation or must be doing something. For the few moments you take to sit quietly, there is nothing to do, no place to go, no one to see or call or respond to, no plan or idea to think about, no money to earn, no boss to appease or employee to supervise, no partner to support or discuss something with, no kids to feed or chase.

No, there is only you, and you don't want to bother or

disturb yourself with anything. For fifteen minutes or so today, you are as close to inert matter as you can be. And if you can manage to incorporate this into your everyday life, the calm centeredness will connect you with the love that already exists within you and around you.

Day sixteen Write down the personal qualities you would like to develop, and see them as your current goals. It doesn't matter whether you feel these are practical or realistic, or whether at this point you have any confidence that you can achieve them. What matters is that this is what you want to become. Think about what these attributes are and make a list of them. Carry the list with you so you can refer to it easily.

You don't have to do any more than that to begin the process of developing the qualities you have identified. Be specific, and record them in the present tense, as if these characteristics already exist. Do you want to become more refined, more of a gentleman? Do you want to know how to dress appropriately for every occasion in your life, to act and speak with gentility, grace, and style? Write this down. Say, "I am a gentleman, and I am acting with grace, gentility, and style." Would you like to have a better memory? Would it please you to remember names, dates, and places more accurately than you do now? Do you marvel at the way some people can recollect the past and remember specific sentences from actual conversations that may have taken place years ago? Write that down: "I am re-membering all the names, faces, and stories of the people I meet."

If you are serious about wanting to be in a significant relationship, include that in your list. If you are really se-rious about it, inscribe nothing else, because this will focus your attention on what really matters to you, and if it's only one thing, it will send a message to the universe that you have no desire right now for anything but a loving, supportive relationship. Write it positively: "I am thriving in a committed, enduring relationship in which we mutu-ally honor, respect, and support each other."

Consult your list frequently. You can state aloud what you have written as a more powerful way of affirming what you want to happen in your life. You are the creator. You steer your own course. If you want to be more satisfied with what you already have, you can do that. If you want to slow down and appreciate the time you spend with your kids, that can be done as well. *Let it be easy.* Start by writing it down.

Day seventeen   Try something new. If you've never been to a baseball game, call a friend and go out to the ballpark. Have you ever baked a cake, visited Paris or the Smoky Mountains, painted your bathroom, attended a Grateful Dead concert, or changed a diaper? Try it, or at least begin to plan to try it if it's not easily accomplished today.

What does it feel like to be in strange situations, with rhythms, behaviors, and attitudes that are completely foreign to you? Is the game of baseball more exciting than you thought it would be—because you are sitting in the stands with a bag of peanuts and a cup of cold beer—or less so? How does it feel to be in a place where your native language is not spoken, or to be among mountain vistas and lush forests? What changes in your sense of self do you detect? Does this new environment encourage you to see the world differently?

Spend the night on the couch in your living room. If you drink coffee in the morning, start today with a cup of tea, or a glass of grapefruit juice instead of your customary orange. Become aware of who you normally are by doing something you don't normally do. Take note of how you feel, how comfortable you are with change, whether you welcome or fear new things.

The Mystery of the Natural World

One of the legacies of the Scientific Revolution of the seventeenth century is that we view nature as something to control—and to a great extent we have succeeded in doing so. But the results are decidedly mixed. It's difficult to imagine such early modern thinkers as Galileo, Francis Bacon, or Descartes, who believed our destiny was to conquer the natural world, approving of the present condition of the planet. In fact, I have wondered if they would have gone back to the drawing board if they had been able to see the future— a world in which pollution and general environmental degradation confront us everywhere we turn.

I maintain that in order to have a nurturing, loving life on the human level it is essential to extend that love to nature itself, and that means experiencing the stunning array of natural processes directly. Those who do not see the earth as their home, as the place from which every single moment of their lives springs, are cutting off a part of themselves and suffering the consequences, even if they are not aware of them directly. For nature is us, too.

It is not something separate that we turn to when we want something to grow or to be removed from our path, or used in some way for our personal benefit. As in our intimate relationships with one another, we must learn to be respectful of our surroundings and let go of trying to "tame" everything we encounter.

It has always struck me as the ultimate in human arrogance that we even talk about the conquest of nature, as if nature were an enemy to be subdued in battle. Such expressions also indicate how language guides our thinking. If we live our lives in terms of victory and defeat, of winners and losers, then conquest is a natural outgrowth of what we do. We want something; we go after it.

But if we want to live in peace and harmony—to, in effect, have more love in our lives—we must live in accordance with the laws of nature. These laws are revealed to us in a multitude of ways—through human and animal development, the changing seasons, or the earth's diverse terrain—and we must change not only our way of thinking but our very language. The only things left to "conquer" before we can forever do away with this entire mindset are violence and ignorance, and the only way we can accomplish this ambitious agenda is through love and understanding. This task begins with the natural world, of which we are a vital part.

To be sure, there is cause for hope. Environmental consciousness has recently become as much a part of the political landscape as concerns about the economy or safe streets, for we intuitively recognize that we cannot go on indefinitely bespoiling our ecosystem in the name of "progress." It's no secret that if less-developed nations were to industrialize to the extent that we in the West have, the earth could not take it. Our planet cannot bear the burden of billions more people brought into the industrialized way of life. We must find another path.

And that path, to me, begins with love. It is obviously no substitute for diligent and thoughtful research, critical thinking, a willingness to compromise, trial and error, and the application of moral and political suasion, but it is certainly the glue that binds all these together. Love seeks to unite, to include, to treat all else and all others as we want to be treated. Love is the wellspring of creativity that can heal the wounds of our planet; that can make peace among nations, peoples, and on the streets of our own land; that can bring the way we live into harmony with what Mother Earth can provide us; and that can fulfill the utopian dream of the ages, which is to create a Peaceable Kingdom where the lion shall truly lie down with the lamb.

Progress no longer means the conquest of nature —or the conquest of anybody or anything. Progress means finding a way to live a balanced life, both globally and locally. And for many of us who want to contribute to a peaceful, just, safe, and clean world, I would suggest that we broaden the message of the popular bumper sticker: "Think universally, act personally."

Day one Spend time in a flower garden. Stay there as long as you wish, but make sure your visit is long enough to take in the various charms that the world of blossoms and petals provides. You can sit in a chair or on the grass, lie down looking up at the flowers from below, or walk around. However you choose to spend your time, be aware that you are a guest in someone else's home— nature's—so act accordingly.

If the day is warm and sunny, savor the rays and imagine how the flowers must feel at this very moment. Look closely at the variety of blooms, at the different shapes and colors, at the way the individual blossoms grow out of their leafy sheaths. Now use your sense of smell to take in the stunning array of fragrance, all of which can be divinely overpowering.

Keep an eye out for the various animal life that also lives in the garden, the birds and squirrels, the insects that fly, the ones that crawl. Notice how intently they go about their business, how they move from place to place trying not to notice you but in fact finding that task difficult. Close your eyes and listen to the sounds of the garden, the chirping and humming, and the movement of the stems and leaves in the mild breeze.

Now see if you can transcend your individual senses and feel the presence of the garden inside you. Try to become just another flower, at home in the garden as if you were in your own house or place of worship. Can you let go of your humanness for a time and transform your existence into something else? Can you lose yourself in a place that men and women have celebrated since time immemorial? What does it feel like to be a flower, to be the object of affection of a bee?

Day two   Go camping. Just take off on the spur of the moment, or plan a more elaborate trip if you are so inclined, but do whatever you have to do to get out in nature for an extended period of time. Try to take as little as you can along with you. Leave the battery-operated television and your beeper at home.

Find out why nature still inspires and satisfies most of us who experience it, why its beauty, serenity, perfection, and ways of life suffuse our consciousness. Think of how poets and artists throughout the ages have been moved to write, paint, draw, and sculpt by the unique ways in which nature inspired them, how every hundred years or so an artistic movement arises that bases its concepts on the wondrous mysteries of the natural world.

You can get close to all this just by spending a few days camping with your friends, your family, or by yourself. You can wake up with the sun and cook your meals on a small outdoor stove you bring along. Many people are not more than a few hours from a lovely little spot that will provide you with all the inspiration you require to get the most out of your venture. Within minutes of your departure, your daily cares will be behind you, and all that awaits is the slower, more deliberate pace of the world of plants and animals.

Day three   Spend some time with the sun. You can begin by waking up early to watch the sun rise, to see it as it slowly creeps up over the eastern horizon and begins its twelve-hour journey across the heavens. Don't look at the sun directly, of course. It might be fun to invite a friend or your partner or child to come along with you. Bring a warm beverage and some food, and make an early-morning picnic out of your adventure.

During the day, stay outdoors in the bright sunshine as much as you can. Wear sunscreen and cover the parts of your body that are unaccustomed to the exposure, but see if you can play all day. You can take long walks, garden, make "sun tea," find a park bench and read a book or magazine, or wear portable headphones and listen to Beethoven's Ninth or to New Age music. Or you can take along a comfortable chair, find a nice, quiet spot away from the madding crowd, and indulge in my favorite sun activity— a nap.

At the end of the day, if you still have energy and want to complete your spell in the sun, go out and watch the sunset with someone special. Discuss your feelings about nature and what your favorite experiences of the day were. Are you invigorated? Have you taken in the full effects of our bright star? Now, if you're so inclined, write down your observations of the day. Or make brief notes and save the flowery prose for another time, turning it into a letter that you send to a loved one close by or far away.

Day four   Think of yourself as an animal. Imagine life as a member of another species. There are no limitations. How do you see yourself? Are you a lion, the undisputed champion of the animal kingdom? Or are you a dog that gets to run wild on a beach, jumping into the water to fetch a stick, following the rhythm of the waves again and again? How about an eagle, with sharp eyes and wide, graceful wings, able to see all from a position high above the rest? Which animal would you be?

Each species has things going for it. Bears get to sleep all winter and don't have to deal with cold temperatures and a scarcity of food. Giraffes have no difficulty reaching sweet leaves on tall trees. But each species also has its disadvantages. If you were a porcupine, people wouldn't want to come near you. And if you decided to become an elephant, you might be big and powerful, but if you were a female you'd have to be pregnant for nearly two years if you wanted to give birth.

I used to want to be an eagle. I used to dream of being above it all, having the means to cover a lot of territory quickly, swooping down to get involved in what looked promising whenever I chose, then lifting myself out again to perch closer to the stars. But now I'm not so sure. There is something about a turtle that appeals to me. They are very slow and deliberate, but as every child or child-at-heart knows, they eventually win the race. They have a hard exterior—they have to, since they can't outrun anyone—but they are squishy soft on the inside.

I would never want to be a beaver—all that work building dams from morning till night. I think a cat would be a good choice. They don't waste any time or energy. They take naps in sunny spots whenever they can. They seem to get what they want, have soft, furry coats, and like to curl up with whoever is nearby. But that terrible catfood!

Day five Expose yourself to extremes. Get in touch with the full force of nature, within reason. Don't do anything that will jeopardize your safety, but try to move out of your climatic comfort zone by letting the power of the elements alter the way you feel. See how your body responds to different meteorological conditions.

Although it's summer and the temperatures tend to be warm, see if you can watch for the approach of a storm, a thundershower perhaps, or at least rainy and windy conditions, and spend time in them. If you are willing to get wet, go out in the rain and slosh around a bit, feeling what it's like to get pelted by raindrops and buffeted by the wind. If a thunderstorm does develop, get as close to it as you can. Imagine for a moment that you have just arrived from a planet where there are no rainstorms and experience the storm as that person. See if you can feel the electricity in the air as the dark cloud envelops you and heavy rains fall all around you.

Another way to experience the variety of natural conditions is to plunge yourself into bodies of water that vary in temperature. If there is a spa nearby that has a warm pool, get into it for a while, then get out and take a brief cold shower before plunging back into the warm water. See how your body reacts to this. Feel the extremes as they penetrate your consciousness and remind you of the variety of conditions that are found in nature, which are equivalent to the various moods, feelings, and emotional states that are found in us humans.

Your relationship to the natural world is no different from any other relationship you have. There are extremes to which you sometimes have to respond. Most of the time, however, things are pretty temperate, if you are adaptable and learn to accept what you cannot control.

Day six   Visit a natural history or science museum. If there is one in your city or town, spend some time there. See what kinds of exhibits are available to you, the glimpses of nature that professional museum experts choose to display for your enlightenment and enjoyment. Do they create natural habitats that would be difficult for you to see otherwise? Are there exhibits of dinosaurs that give you an idea of what life on earth was like millions of years ago?

If you don't live close to a museum of this kind, make plans to visit one when you have the opportunity. Bring children along with you. They usually have a lively curiosity about nature and will be fascinated by the displays. You'll see how a child relates to the natural world, and how you once saw it as well.

When I was a small boy, I frequently visited the Franklin Institute in Philadelphia—sometimes as often as once a week. My visits kindled an interest in the natural world that persists even today. I remember walking through a replica of a human heart that was just about the most interesting thing I could ever imagine.

You will be exposed to aspects of nature you might never have known, or once knew and have forgotten. Think about how you fit in. Do you feel superior to all these forms, or just another part of a vast network of plant and animal life that is mutually interdependent? How is this a metaphor for your own relationships?

Day seven   Watch a baby being born, if you really want to immerse yourself in the world of nature. It might not be easy to gain access to something so personal, but try. Talk to a Lamaze teacher or hospital worker and volunteer to be a coach for a single mother. Or borrow a videotape of women giving birth. If the idea of witnessing a human birth makes you squeamish, visit a farm or stable and watch a calf or foal being born.

Imagine how many times this event has been repeated since the beginning of time. Think about the various stages of labor and delivery, how the body knows when the infant is ready for the world, able to exist on its own. Watching a live birth, especially if you've never seen one before, will probably give you an insight into nature that you could never have received any other way.

Think of how much better it is today to have husbands in delivery rooms. For me, the births of my sons remain among my most vivid and emotional memories—the controlled excitement, the intense work of assistance, the excruciatingly slow process, the surfeit of bodily fluids, the relief, and then the exhilaration. Think of how far we've come since the days when fathers wore out the soles of their shoes pacing hospital waiting rooms, and then passed out cigars when their babies were born.

We've also come a long way since mothers were completely anesthetized and then awakened hours later and given their babies to hold. We now have a closer, more intimate relationship with natural processes, one that enables us to love more passionately. This exposure in the best of circumstances teaches us understanding and empathy, the ability to feel what someone else is feeling and to partake of the entire range of joys and sorrows of life. What better teacher than nature, and what better lesson from nature than the miracle of birth?

Day eight Take care of an animal. It could be your pet, or the dog, cat, turtle, hamster, tropical fish, rabbit, snake, or parrot of a friend or relative. Whatever the circumstances, pay close attention today to the needs of the animal.

Start by becoming aware of the way in which the animal is relating to you. If he or she is your pet, don't take her for granted today. Let her know how much you appreciate her, that you will be extra loving, and that you intend to show your affection in every way possible. That might mean stroking your cat across his back a few hundred times, or playing Frisbee with your dog for two hours, or having a conversation with your parrot well into the evening. Spare no action or display of emotion. You can even tell your turtle how much you love him. Go ahead. In his own way he'll understand what you mean.

If you are not very familiar with animals, ask to borrow your neighbor's dog and take him out for a walk. You can learn in a few minutes what to do, how to hold the leash, how to clean up the mess and properly dispose of it, how to say "good dog" and "sit." Or offer to feed your sister's goldfish, just to see how the fish moves gingerly up to the top of the tank to snare the little morsels of food.

Interacting with an animal is another way to understand your relationship with nature and to see how much potential for love exists all around you. Although each animal displays its affection in a special way, every pet knows when a human being is present and attentive.

Contact with animals benefits us as well. Studies clearly demonstrate that elderly people who have a dog or cat are happier and healthier and live longer than those who live alone. The connection is evident. The natural world can be an abiding source of love, affection, and tenderness.

Day nine   Reverse your normal waking and sleeping patterns. If daytime is usually your active time, spend your active time today at night. Be a night owl. You're probably going to have to do some planning to accomplish this, but it can be done. Get some rest in the afternoon and try to be as alert and awake before nightfall as you possibly can be. Enlist a partner in your little experiment. Perhaps your spouse, son, or daughter will volunteer to be your companion as you start your "day" in the evening and go about your business during the night.

Pretend the moon is your sun. When it rises, it's your signal to begin your activities. You can have a bite to eat, listen to music, or go out. You can read on the sofa in the living room, or be outdoors and commune with the stars. If you have someone with you, this is an ideal opportunity to talk about your life in a relaxed and unhurried way. After all, you probably are not going to be interrupted by ringing telephones or other obligations. And the unusualness of your endeavor should trigger a fresh perspective on your life. Why not take advantage of this opportunity?

Get in touch with the energy of night, the pace and rhythm and overall feeling of spending your waking time in darkness. Think of how different nocturnal animals are—raccoons, owls. Think of how different life is for people who work the night shift in restaurants, parking garages, hospitals, and bakeries. How comfortable are you with all this? Can you adapt to the nighttime world in which you are normally asleep? Do you have trouble staying awake, or do you have the energy and the will to go on for hours, doing whatever comes naturally to you?

Are you a night person or a morning person? Or perhaps an afternoon person? When are you most productive, creative, and energetic? Can you allow your natural rhythm to come forth? Is there an inherent connection between daylight and activity, and darkness and sleep? What about people who live in the extreme northern or southern parts of the world, where days are often either all light or all dark? What do you think they do to adjust? Do you think you could live there and adapt?

Day ten   Preserve something. It doesn't matter what it is. It could be something natural, like a plant or bush, or a little nest of birds that has made a home in your backyard, or a park in your city or town that needs restoration and could use a contribution.

Learn about the impulse to sustain, the entire series of questions that the environmental movement has raised. What is worth preserving, and why? How much do you value the natural world around you—the air, water, and land that provide you with what you need every day to grow and prosper? Imagine for a moment that these elements were in danger of disappearing altogether, and you were forced to spend your days not enjoying your leisure or being productive at work but calling around to find some clean water to drink, air to breathe, or land to live on that is not contaminated with industrial waste.

When you preserve something, when you plant a flower or a tree and water it, expose it to sunshine, care for it, and protect it against animals that might want to eat or destroy it, you understand what is precious about the world around us, what is irreplaceable, what cannot ultimately be created by us in a laboratory. Spend the day trying to keep things exactly as they are—to avoid walking on the grass, swatting a fly, or pulling a flower from its stem, and also avoid the overpackaged and overprocessed consumer items that destroy the environment in unseen ways.

Or you might decide today to sit down and write a generous check to a group that is working diligently to preserve something that you cherish, whether it's a nearby meadow that a neighborhood association is trying to keep from being developed, or the oceans, which an international organization is working to clean up. Find out more about the environmental or conservation movements in general, and what they are doing to preserve the natural habitat. Certainly one group will reflect your overall political views. Find out what it thinks is worth preserving.

$\mathcal{D}$ay eleven Spend the day with water. Discover more about how this basic element of life works. See how it feels to be near water, to be in water, to have water as your constant companion. Think of as many ways as you can to have water interact with your body. Drink it, bathe in it, swim in it, wash your car or your dog, cook something using water, make ice cubes. Or you can get into a Jacuzzi, or engage in vigorous physical exercise and work up a big sweat.

See if you can be more comfortable with water at the end of today than you were at the beginning. If you are already at ease with it, come up with creative ways to know it better, to understand its properties. In spas throughout Europe, people take water "cures," and European insurance companies pay for people to absorb the healing properties of water at these remarkable natural springs.

If you live near a large body of water, visit it today. You can float on a raft or in a tube, with a magazine and a cool glass of lemonade or iced tea. Or sit by a lake or the ocean and watch the way water behaves when there is a lot of it, the way it moves about audaciously and challenges you to see if you have the courage to get near or in it. Watch the waves hit the shore with tremendous force, only to rush back and play their eternal song once again.

If it happens to rain today, pay particular attention to the way everything around you changes. Watch as the sky darkens, the air takes on a different smell, and the moisture all around you increases. Suddenly you can feel the drops falling on your face and the rest of your body. Spend time in the rain shower watching the earth almost break into a smile as it thanks the universe for this satisfying, thirst-quenching drink of water.

Day twelve   Look for a rainbow. Spend the day in hot pursuit of this most colorful of nature's displays. If the day dawns absolutely clear, with bright sunshine that threatens to last for the foreseeable future, spray your hose gently, or wait until rain comes again, with the possibility that light will refract and form the spectrum of all colors.

A rainbow I saw recently was one of the most awesome things I've ever encountered. I was totally mesmerized by the perfect, vivid arc that extended from one hill to another, above a freeway taking commuters home. I realized that I had never seen a real rainbow until I saw this one, and I'll never forget the sight. Was there a pot of gold at the end of this rainbow? No, there wasn't. Have you ever met anyone who has actually seen this famous pot? I haven't either, but there must be some truth to it or people wouldn't have passed down the myth to our generation.

Maybe the pot of gold is the rainbow itself, its colorful promise of the possibilities that life offers.

Did you ever try to watch water boil? It's almost impossible. You can't identify the moment bubbles start erupting because you are looking too closely. It's the same with rainbows. Nature doesn't like to be watched too carefully. The natural world is modest. It prefers to bestow its charms on those who are worthy, because of the way they are with other people, animals, and especially children. So if you are looking for a rainbow, the best thing you can do is take a small child on a train ride through varying terrain, or on a trip to a waterfall.

Day thirteen Visit the wilderness. Earlier in the month, I suggested that you go camping. Today, we are upping the ante by going way off the beaten track and into parts of this earth that are not regularly seen by human eyes. Plan a trip to God's country.

If you don't live close to any wilderness areas, see if you can make some time in your schedule to get there. A mountainous terrain is probably best because it is somewhat difficult to reach and thus more pristine. Find the most remote spot possible, and then hike into this place where cars, off-track vehicles, and even loggers don't venture. It may take you two or three hours to get there, but once you've arrived, you'll know it.

How will you know it? By the near silence, by the sound

of the wind blowing freely. You'll know it by the vast and open terrain, by the size of everything, by the way the sky looks as it meets the earth. Time will seem to melt away, movement will take on a pace of its own, appropriate to the basic elements of natural life—earth, air, water, and the products of their combination. When you return to your everyday life, you'll realize how arbitrary your notion of time is, how focused it is on working and getting many things accomplished, and how the wilderness must laugh behind our backs at the hurried, harried pace of our lives.

Finally, you'll know you are in the wilderness by how small you feel, how tiny you seem in comparison to the vastness of the mountains. All around you are a few million trees extending as far as the eye can see; you may stumble on a pond that looks as if it's so deep it could go all the way down to the center of the earth. You can almost hear the world of the wilderness telling you to go back and do whatever you can to take care of what remains of its perfection.

Regardless of what you think when you return, your trip to the wilderness will leave its mark on you. I don't know anyone who has ever witnessed the majesty of undisturbed nature and not been moved.

Day fourteen   Choose your own path. Making your own trail in the wilderness is a no-no, but in life it's the only way to go.

In fact, the natural world requires it. If you observe for any length of time the comings and goings of animal life, you'll see that the function of the parents is to prepare the young for an independent existence, that at some point all the cubs, the kittens, or the pups will have to fend for themselves. It's the same way with human beings, although somehow we've extended the period of dependency long beyond its usefulness. Freud attributed part of the cause of human neurosis to the fact that we are emotionally dependent on our mothers and fathers long after we are biologically capable of independence.

Well, today is the day you can start to be more consistent with nature by choosing your own path, by deciding that your uniqueness as an individual requires that you be you. Even if you look like someone else, talk like someone else, act like someone else, think like someone else, work like someone else, or play like someone else, you are you, and you are on your own course. Others may help you, guide you, persuade you, influence you, hinder you, try to stop you, or lay traps along the way, but all this is of no avail. You are going to continue down the path you choose, a path that, regardless of twists and turns, you will continually recognize as your path.

Keep in mind that your way will pass through all kinds of terrain and that at times you will be alone and at other times someone will be with you. At certain moments you will be responsible for other people on your path, and at other moments they will take care of you. There will be uphills, downhills, and many occasions where there is no hill at all. You will feel strong during some periods and weak during others, and after a while on your trail, you will sense when to slow down and when to pick up the pace, when to rest and when to move ahead.

But whatever happens along the way, the fundamental truth is that you have freely chosen this path, this life, this love, and that as long as you are a fully functioning human being, with a will and an ability to respond to circumstances that develop along the way, you are safe. You are prepared for whatever happens. You will be like the old Zen master, who recognized finally that his attempt to outrun a hungry bear was going to be unsuccessful, and who jumped off a cliff in order to avoid being devoured. He hung onto a small tree branch trying to stave off the inevitable, reached for a plump, wild strawberry, and remarked, "What a delicious strawberry!"

Fall

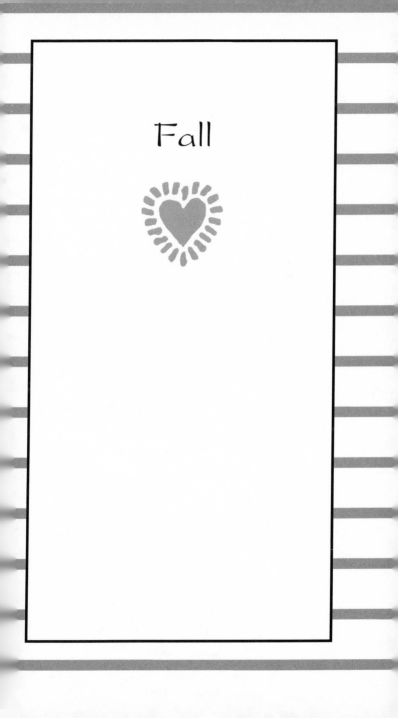

Deepening Friendship and a Sense of Community

When I was growing up, I was part of an extended family that included aunts, uncles, cousins, grandparents, and family friends who were often called Uncle and Aunt. This extended family was my domestic reality. We lived with my maternal grandmother until I was thirteen, and numerous relatives lived within a mile of my home, which was the family gathering place on Sundays. I had a lot of people to observe and contemplate—great political debates between the Republican and Democratic factions of the family, meals we all shared, lazy summer afternoons with the baseball game playing on the radio in the background, and a great deal of attention from a variety of adults.

Today this scenario is rare. People are scattered, far afield. Economic demands and basic American wanderlust have disrupted the geographical proximity of families and compelled people to look to friends and a wider community for the kind of emotional sustenance that used to take place only within families. The prevalence of therapy and the rise of the helping professions in general come from two sources—the increase in discretionary income and the absence of family members close by who can listen with empathy and provide wise counsel. It used to be common for an aunt, older cousin, or grandparent to offer his or her considerable wisdom to younger people, but now we depend on professionals and friends to fulfill these needs because our family is far away.

I've noticed that this is to some degree a generational difference. My age group relies much more heavily on friends and community for love—in the form of support groups and other associations—than our parents ever did. My parents marvel at how wonderful my friends are, how devoted, how much we have shared together—our joys and sorrows, successes and triumphs. And in fact I feel very fortunate to have close, dear friends I've known for nearly thirty years, people who delight in me, and vice versa.

What it takes to have a lot of love in your life from friendships and other associations is simple: attention. There is no substitute for investing energy in a relationship, for staying in touch when people are far away, for getting together when people are nearby, for sharing the true essence of your life rather than glossing over reality with superficialities.

If you know how to be a friend, or to involve yourself in the work or ethic of a community of people, then you know how to love. You connect. You put out energy. You take the time—however little your busy life allows—to keep up your end of relationships with a phone call, letter, or occasional visit. You derive love and affection *from* these relationships because you offer love and affection *to* these relationships. The love you feel for a friend comes from the same source as the love you feel for a child, an intimate partner, a mother or brother. It just takes a different form.

$\mathcal{D}$ay one Start a tradition with a friend. A pleasant routine could just spring up over time, or you and your friend could deliberately decide to start a tradition. Either way, make sure you acknowledge that each of you will do his or her part in keeping the tradition alive.

Whenever you get together with this particular friend, meet at the same place. It could be at a restaurant for lunch, or at a delightful park for a stroll around the lake, or at your home to listen to classical music. You might want to switch and go to your friend's house on occasion, as long as something is the same when the two of you get together, and you are aware that you are doing things in the customary way.

This idea goes back a long way for me. I go to baseball games with one friend. For a long time we went to day games. He drove; I made sandwiches. Now we mostly find ourselves at night games on Mondays. We meet at his office, he drives, and we have dinner in the same restaurant before the game. (We even try to get the same table if we can.) With another friend, I always have lunch in the same diner. (He orders the same thing every time; I don't.)

My wife and I go to a particular restaurant every year on our wedding anniversary—and never go there at any other time. And if I think about it, I have small traditions with most of my friends. It's these little remembrances and benchmarks that define who and what we are to each other.

$\mathcal{D}$ay two   Stay in touch with a friend by making a tape to send to him or her. It's easier to make an audiotape, but if you're feeling ambitious and want to use a video camera, feel free. This friend can be someone with whom you haven't corresponded recently, or someone you talked to last week. That's not important. What matters is that you feel the desire to communicate with this person.

I did this successfully with one buddy. For years we taped hour-long conversations for each other, and although we now use the telephone I still have his tapes—from the seventies—and from time to time I listen to one or two. They are fascinating reminders of times gone by. They are also cultural and social scrapbooks. I tune into music I once loved, and hear him discuss topics that were important in my twenties.

To start out, just sit down in a comfortable spot with a recorder and a fresh tape. Turn it on and start talking. I used to begin my tapes with some music I liked at the time. When I wanted to pause for a moment, I simply turned off the machine and waited until I felt like continuing. Sometimes, it took a few sittings to complete the tape, but usually I had no problem speaking into the microphone for an hour.

If you want to have loving friendships, there is no substitute for time and attention. Sometimes, given our busy world, it's easier to talk into a machine than it is to write a letter. You can also elaborate more easily on an idea or issue, and your friend has the pleasure of hearing your voice as well as your words. It's a lovely way to communicate, and it's easy to make it a tradition.

Day three   Throw a party. This is a great way to connect with all your friends at the same time, and to offer them the opportunity to meet people they've probably heard about for years. It's also a way to demonstrate your fine sense of hospitality, to show your willingness to extend yourself, and to show the universe that friendship is important to you.

Of course, when you put together the guest list, you'll want to invite both new and old friends, so that everyone will have a chance to mingle and talk to one another. Pretend you are a teenager and this party is an important milestone. You might want to have a theme, like a funny-hat party or a flashy-jewelry party, or perhaps an exotic-foods party.

If the weather permits, have the party outdoors. Try to arrange this at your home. If you can't, consider a local park and make the party a picnic, with volleyball, horse-shoes, or badminton as the principal physical activity.

Don't expect to spend much time with any one of your friends. As the host, you'll probably be too busy to have many long conversations. The point is to gather in one place the friends who mean so much to you, to be among all of them, to introduce them to one another, to be surrounded with loving energy and goodwill, and to honor your guests with your careful consideration and attention. The expense of the party is not important. In fact, you can even have a potluck affair. What matters is the love with which you go about planning the celebration and what you bring to each aspect of it, whether it's the food, the design, the music, the games, or the choice of guests, as well as your own attitude and ability to be the host of the party.

$\mathcal{D}$ay four   Collaborate on a project, whether it is an errand a friend needs to run or a task around the house you've been meaning to do. It can be something large, like adding a new staircase to your back porch or redecorating your child's bedroom, or something small, like getting all your cans, bottles, and newspapers together for recycling, or trimming your hedges. The point is to carry out the activity together, to help each other while you deepen your friendship.

Working together is an ideal time to share thoughts and feelings about what's going on in your lives, as you accomplish the job that's before you. Take the time to connect, working side by side with your friend to complete more efficiently the task you have chosen to do.

Make sure you are aware of how precious this time is, how privileged you are to have a friend who will collaborate with you. If you are the one who is receiving the help, ask this person how he or she wants to be acknowledged for it. If your friend refuses any gift, insist. Take him or her out for a meal at her favorite restaurant. Buy a small gift as a token of your appreciation. This is an opportunity to deepen your friendship. If you are the helper, perform your tasks cheerfully, out of kindness and generosity, without expecting anything in return. You may be surprised at how grateful your friend is.

Friendship can be an area in your life from which you can derive a lot of love—if you are choosing the right people as friends, those who can appreciate your gifts and are willing to share themselves with you.

Day five Discuss a hot political issue. Get together with a friend or acquaintance, or a few of them, and talk about a current event, or an idea that has been in the news recently. It could be something happening locally, nationally, or internationally. It could even be an event that happened long ago that is being reinterpreted. What matters is that you and your companions can really allow one another to express your views fully and passionately.

You can meet in one of your homes or go to a public place, like a café or a park or the lobby of a nearby hotel. Leave yourselves enough time to allow everyone to be heard. Although you can skip from topic to topic, as the Sunday news talk shows do, try to be more polite than those commentators are and let someone finish his or her thought before interrupting.

Turn this into an exercise in listening. If you disagree with someone, state your opinion firmly but cordially, explaining why you see a particular issue in a different light. Ask your friend for clarification. Have him or her explain his views to you more fully, so that you can understand the logic of his thinking. Illustrate your points with examples. If you feel that Republicans are better for the economy, say why. If you feel that the Democrats have better ideas on how to create more jobs, give examples.

Keep in mind also that this is an exercise in democracy, that the foundation of personal freedom lies in the exchange of ideas between people, that what separates us from dictatorships and other forms of totalitarianism is that we can participate in the political process. This is the essence of the democratic process, ordinary people examining important issues—beginning with discussions among friends.

Day six   Introduce yourself to someone new. If for any reason a man or woman interests you, go ahead, make contact. It could be the way she smiles or how he wears his hair. It's possible that you are meeting this person for the first time, or that you see or run into him more frequently, perhaps on a regular basis. Regardless of the circumstances, if you would like to find out if you could be friends with this person, take a risk. Walk up to him or her and say, "Hi. I've noticed you a number of times now. My name is Anthony Green, what's yours?"

Chances are this person will be impressed with your charm, courage, and friendly manner and will respond in kind. Some cultures would, of course, consider this move inappropriate, but ours isn't one of them. We reward audacity. If you have the time, strike up a conversation with this man or woman, exchanging pleasantries about the weather or events going on in your town. If you know you will see him again, you don't even have to get his telephone number on this occasion. You can wait until you've reflected on your brief encounter. If you think you do want to get together, exchange numbers. Offer to call and do so.

Some of my very best friendships have come about because of my initiative. If you have a hunch that you may like a person, chances are he or she will like you, too. Right there you have a basis for friendship.

The key word is action. You have to take the lead. No one in the world has a lot of good friends without acting —sometimes on impulse—to make contact and then to build on what he or she begins. Your relationship doesn't have to be heavy or intense, and your time together can consist of an occasional cup of tea or a tennis match.

Making friends is an art form, and it involves some risk. But the saying "Nothing ventured, nothing gained" is crucial here. Without making overtures, it is difficult to make friends. The first step is to introduce yourself. And make sure you smile as you do.

$\mathcal{D}$ay seven   Be a healer. Go out of your way today to see a friend, relative, or acquaintance who feels wounded, bring people together who are having problems, shed light on difficulties that either you or others may be having of late, or be of comfort to someone who is bereaved, in need, or in physical or emotional turmoil. So much of having more love in your life through your involvement with friends and community means building a loving network around you, and that so often means reaching out to people who are hurting in some way and offering to assist in their healing.

This doesn't mean playing doctor, religious leader, or therapist. Leave that to people who are trained in these areas. It does mean being a human being, extending yourself, letting people know that you care, that you understand, that you are willing to listen, that they will have your full and active attention for whatever time you have to spare. You can't be Mother Teresa and give, give, give. But you can be yourself and give.

You also don't have to try to solve every problem today—just be fully present. Is a friend or neighbor having some difficulty with a wayward teenager? Offer to mediate, at least to listen to both sides dispassionately. Is there an elderly woman in your community whose screen door needs to be repaired so her cat won't get out? Fix it, or arrange for someone else to do it if you don't have the time. Is someone you know pained by the impending death of a loved one—a friend, parent, or partner? Try to make it better for him or her by asking what you can do to ease his burden. Make an extra pot of soup and bring it over, freeze a week's worth of homemade meals, or offer to watch his kids.

When you see yourself as a healer, as someone who is willing to extend herself for the sake of other people, you create personal community and increase the quality of love in your life at the same time. You are part of what some non-Western peoples call the "long body," an extension of the personal self to the other selves around you.

Day eight Investigate another religion. Find out something about someone else's faith so you can understand how other people think or live, and also understand your own life more fully by noting the differences. You may also feel a stronger connection to your larger community by knowing more about the beliefs of so many of its members.

There are a variety of ways of doing this. You can talk to someone who practices another religion, read a book or two that explains and clarifies certain issues that may be of interest to you, talk to a member of the clergy, who might be able to enlighten you, or attend the service of another faith and observe the rituals and listen to the sermon. Try to get in touch with the feelings that come up for you while you are there.

If you are a Protestant, see if you can make arrangements to speak to a Catholic or Jew. Have a number of questions to ask. Try to get at the essentials of the religion, rather than the small, finer points that may be more superficial. See if you can follow one of the dreams of our country's founders, that this would be a place of religious toleration and that all peoples would be able to come here and practice their faiths without interference or persecution. The more you understand the religion and culture of other people, the more tolerant and understanding you personally become.

In my case, growing up Jewish mostly among Jews, I had a deep suspicion of Christianity and anything to do with Jesus. In fact, he was hardly ever mentioned in my house, and I had to endure the sting of anti-Semitic remarks directed at me by the kids who attended the local Catholic school and rode the bus with me. It wasn't until I was a graduate student in my twenties, studying European history, that I began to have an appreciation for the more sublime, loving, and charitable aspects of the Christian religion. And then Nikos Kazantzakis's book *The Last Temptation of Christ* introduced me to Jesus the man. My understanding of Christianity was forever changed.

If you seek to understand the world, the world seeks to understand you. If love is your goal, then you must be comfortable with diversity, and becoming more aware of other faiths and ways of living puts you in very close contact with how other people feel and live and what they aspire to.

Day nine   Join a group. The group can address any one of your interests—just so you can participate with other people in discussions, activities, or projects to heighten and better develop your sense of community. The easiest way to feel connected, to feel more love, even if it's not romantic love but the love of being with people who share something in common with you, is to join or form a group.

The group can be for people who like to prepare a particular kind of food, enjoy reading and talking about good books, want to play Ping-Pong and then go out for a bite and a beverage, or want to promote contacts with people in beleaguered countries abroad or deal with homeless people in this country. The result of your association may be a shelter for those in need, an exchange trip to Eastern Europe, or merely something to increase your passion for life. You may want to found an encouragement group, an association of people who get together to find out what's going on in one another's lives and to offer support to help with following through with plans, dreams, and aspirations.

I have been a member of so many groups I can't remember them all—fraternal groups, political action groups, therapy groups, various book clubs, encouragement groups. What I loved about all of them, whether my involvement lasted six weeks or six years, was that being associated with these people gave me hope, in the profoundest sense. I felt that I wasn't alone, that whatever was going on in my personal life did not constitute the full story, that another part of my life existed, perhaps even a larger part, and that part was connected to people—some of whom I knew only superficially, while others I knew more deeply.

Join a group, and if you don't like that one, try another. Or start a new one! Keep going until you know it's right. You'll feel it.

$\mathcal{D}$ay ten   Visit a neighborhood in which you used to live. Ride up and down the streets in your car, or get out and walk around as you once did. Even if you live on the West Side of Manhattan and you once lived on the East Side of Manhattan, spend the day as if you were still an East Side resident. Relive your old routine. Sometimes you can gain a greater appreciation of your present neighborhood by reacquainting yourself with the one in which you used to live.

What does your old community look like to you now that you don't live there anymore? If you can manage to travel to another city without too much bother, do so. Invite others to go with you. If you have children and they have never seen where you lived when you were single, or never saw the house in which Grandma and Grandpa lived for forty-seven years, show it to them. Point out the school you used to attend, if it's still standing, the yard in which you played ball, or the fence you climbed to get into the local playground at night to kiss Debbie Dunlap in the third grade.

Or you can spend this day alone with your thoughts as you recollect times you spent with certain people in particular places. I did this recently and was very moved by my memories. As I was taking my young son to a baseball game, he fell asleep in the car. I took the opportunity to drive around a neighborhood in San Francisco where I lived for more than seven years. I slowly motored up and down the streets, past my old apartment building, seeing things that used to be part of my daily reality but are now filed away in a memory drawer. I was surprised at how little had changed.

Maybe things are not changing as fast as we think. Or maybe the French have it right when they say that the more things change the more they stay the same. Find out if that's true.

Day eleven   Give away your old clothes. There is no better or easier way to connect with your community than by gathering things you no longer need and dropping them off at a place that will give them to people who can use them.

If you're looking for a way to feel part of a much larger human network, go through your closet, and your husband's and kid's closet, and ask your friends and relatives to do the same. Organize the great giveaway. Buck the trend we read about all the time of people doing things only for money. Forget about the cash you could make by turning this stuff over to a consignment shop. Build a better community by recycling things to people for whom they would be a gift. This is a great way to feel a part of a whole, to understand that you are not an island that exists apart from the mainland but a vital and integral part of a social landscape.

There is undoubtedly someone right at this very moment who is dreaming about wearing your old leather boots, the ones you wore for years until you got a new pair last Christmas. Don't save them for your daughter, who won't get to wear them for three years and probably won't want to wear them anyway. Give them away so that someone can look forward to the coming of cooler weather knowing that she has a great pair of boots to keep her tootsies dry.

Implement the One-Year Rule. If you haven't worn something for a year, chances are you won't ever wear it again (Halloween notwithstanding), and so it's time to give it away. And you'll probably never think about it again.

Day twelve Thank someone for something. Go out of your way today to acknowledge the generosity of a person you know. It doesn't matter if you have known this man or woman your entire life, or have just met him or her and don't know if you will ever see the person again. Thanking him for a service rendered, or a favor given, or for help of some kind will enlarge your personal community to include yet another person.

Do you patronize a business establishment that always provides you with excellent service? Thank the proprietor, or tell an employee how much you appreciate the way you are treated every time you walk in, and ask him to pass the message on to the owner of the business. Or write a quick note to this effect and give it to the person you are talking to.

Thanking someone for a service rendered builds community, as well as friendship. It makes even the most insignificant encounters, like a stranger holding the door for you at the deli, all the more meaningful. It's a way for two people who will probably never know each other's names to connect, even for a moment.

Day thirteen Depend on someone. If you are the type of person who has difficulty letting go of anything you consider to be your responsibility, this is an especially important exercise. It also works well for those who are less concerned about holding on to what they have to do. Today someone else is going to have to come through for you, help you in some way, make a task easier by either doing part of it or accompanying you while you get it done. The idea here is to look to another person as being reliable and dependable.

It may take some time to find the right person for the task. Do you have any heavy furniture to move? Does your car require repairs that mean you will need a ride from the service station to work in the morning, and from work to the service station at the end of the day? Ask someone to help you and make sure you are depending on him or her. Give the man or woman clear instructions about the task. Don't leave anything out. If you need a ride to the doctor's office and would like this person to wait for you, make sure you let him or her know ahead of time. If the wait will be long, perhaps he could do something else and then come back for you.

Learning to depend on people is an important part of a loving life, and the world of friends and community members is a great place to practice this skill. When you rely on other people and they come through for you, it builds confidence. It enables you to see that people are trustworthy, that they are willing to extend themselves or go out of their way for you. And it also creates a bond.

It is a heartfelt experience when someone you are counting on comes through, buys the tickets to the concert as she promised, leaves the front door unlocked since you forgot your key today, lends you a few dollars until the next payday because you are a little short. When you allow yourself to depend on someone else, when you have faith that another person can do something for your benefit, you expand your capacity to love and trust, to put yourself in the hands of another.

Day fourteen Volunteer your time. Decide what cause is most worthy of your attention, and also how much time you have to give—even if it's one hour per month—and donate it. Expect nothing in return, except for the very real reward of the feeling you derive from knowing you have given a gift—freely and without any expectation of anything monetary.

When you volunteer, you are giving one of the most precious elements of your life—your time. You are demonstrating to yourself and to your community that the life you share is important to you. It also enables you to strengthen your ties to your neighbors. The sense of belonging, of being part of a whole that is greater than just yourself or your family, can be deeply satisfying.

In many ways, giving your time is a way to pay back for the gift of life you receive every day, a gift that many of us take for granted. It is a small way of acknowledging that we are part of a large community, that we have much more in common with one another than not. When you volunteer your time, you affirm this.

Start today. Sit down and make a few calls to find out if your chosen organization needs help. They'll be all too glad to accommodate you. In fact, when you appear at their offices, you'll probably be made to feel as if you are the most important person in the world.

Day fifteen Honor your commitments. For one day be a person whose word is his or her bond, who is someone on whom others can depend. Don't make a commitment unless you know you can carry it out, and then let nothing stand in the way of that promise.

Be radical about this. Feel what it's like to know that you have chosen to commit yourself and that you will not let anything deter you. Be on time for meetings and appointments. If you tell your son you will set up trains with him in five minutes, don't take fifteen minutes and pretend you never said five.

Avoid telling people maybe. Maybe is a way of putting things off, and that may be the right thing to do at times, but all too often people use it as an excuse for being indecisive. In fact, when you decide to settle an issue and make a small commitment, it gives you practice and enables you eventually to make greater commitments, like the one to love and honor someone "till death do us part."

There is something sacred about commitments. People who have more love in their lives are people who keep their word, who don't commit to anything unless they are reasonably certain they can follow through. They are also people who are not fearful of commitment, who understand that it is the glue that binds us to one another, that it's in fact one of the bulwarks of civilization itself.

Feeding
the Mind and
Spirit

Watch a small child do anything—piddle around in the dirt, make "scribble-scrabble" on a blank piece of paper, build a tower of Legos—and you see so clearly that learning and play are closely related. To be fully engaged simultaneously with both mind and spirit, to live in the moment, to have no distractions is really what loving, integrated experience is all about. It is so difficult for most people to live this way because they do not know how to rid themselves of their past and future and just be.

Much of the philosophical writing of both East and West talks about the difference between being and doing. Being is the most authentic part of you, the part within. Doing is your output, your production, what you make, what you generate, who you are when you are active and altering the environment around you.

A person will have difficulty either playing or learning—feeding her mind and spirit—when the balance between being and doing is far off center, when being or doing dominates. When "being" dominates "doing," a person is likely to be passive, un-ambitious, lost in contemplation or meditation, indecisive, hypersensitive, or unaware of the world around her. Spirit cannot be nourished because she is living primarily inside, unable to unfold enough to interact with the world outside.

On the other hand, a person who is mostly doing is mostly reacting, cannot focus on what endures, flits from situation to situation without much commitment or depth, and cannot manifest spirit because he is addicted to the external. He is all periphery and no core. He flips through channel after channel on the television trying to find the perfect show or commercial, goes from relationship to relationship in search of the "perfect" partner, and fills his life with activities because his lack of self—of being—makes it uncomfortable for him to be alone with nothing to do.

Ours is a culture of achievement, of doing. We are not likely to have too much being and not enough doing. We are told from the earliest moments of childhood, through school and beyond, to keep busy, get things done, make our mark, move on to the next step, accumulate more possessions—all of which is focused on changing our environments to suit our purposes. We have little encouragement for being, for exploring the world of integrated mind/body/spirit, for taking our time, for waiting patiently for desired results to materialize after much work and discipline, for sitting quietly lost in our own thoughts. Because as a culture we dismiss so cavalierly the thinker, the meditator, the be-er, we often do not realize that spirit must be nourished as well.

People who have the greatest amount of love in their lives are those who can both play and learn. They expose themselves—both their inner and outer lives—to experience. They do not fear change. They see every day as a gift, out of which they fashion the most pleasure, satisfaction, and fulfillment they possibly can. And because they live in order to discover, to explore, to enlarge their comfort zones, to reach into parts of themselves that need developing, they transform their days into opportunities to find out more about this awesome mystery called life.

Learning is not confined to the classroom, or to children, teenagers, and college students. Learning is a lifelong process, a discipline, a devotion to constantly searching for attitudes, beliefs, and behaviors that ultimately contribute to your health and well-being. The ability to love, to connect, to attract, depends on your willingness to nourish both your mind and your spirit. It is much easier to have love if your life is devoted to letting in new things, since life and love are intimately connected, and all life is change.

In the West we learn to rely on our rational minds far too much and on our hearts far too little. I have no quarrel with the mind as a tool. In fact, I have spent my entire life developing my mental and intellectual faculties. But ultimately it is not through the mind alone that the greatest lessons in life are learned—spirit also plays a significant role.

This is why play, at least for me, is the highest, most evolved form of human activity. If you don't know how to play it is very difficult to engage your spirit or know how to learn. The ability to play represents the integration of being and doing, action and contemplation. It is concentration without purpose—other than to receive whatever rewards can be derived from the concentration itself. When I see toddlers at play, their enjoyment doesn't depend on whether they are handling a fancy toy or a large wooden spoon. They could not imagine being anywhere else, not because this particular moment is so special but because no other exists.

If you learn to engage your entire being, to see your life as an opportunity to grow and evolve, to become more aware of yourself, your surroundings, and life itself, then you will have fulfilled the highest form of human existence yet imagined, as set out by Socrates 2,500 years ago—to "know thyself."

$\mathcal{D}ay\ one$ Look at the big picture. If you want to assess a situation, look at the entire context, not at each "fact." If you are having trouble at work, if you are unhappy with what you're doing and a part of you feels you could be prospering in another situation, the big picture tells you not to focus on your discontent but to see it as a sign that you must move on. The big picture will tell you to start planning now for your eventual move, to learn what you can from your present situation, knowing it is not permanent and that a change is in the offing.

Are you having problems with your relationship? Is it lackluster, not providing you with the satisfaction you thought it would, or the satisfaction it once did? Look at the big picture. See the relationship as a learning experience. If some individual moments are painful—if you are bickering, avoiding contact, or casting angry or forlorn looks at each other—broaden the lens. How are you contributing to the friction? How can you adjust your attitude or behavior to mitigate the tension? Examine what this person means to you in the broader context of your life. Can you find what is working and attempt to build the relationship around that? If not, can you take what you have learned with you to the next relationship, whenever that might be?

The choice is yours. You can elect to look at each event in your life and focus on that alone, or you can look at the big picture and try to draw meaning from that. Each life, regardless of where or when it's been lived, has had good and bad days, weeks, months, perhaps even years. The question is, what kind of *life* are you having? That's looking at the big picture, and just asking the question itself probably indicates you're having a good one, or at least one that is better than you may think.

Day two   Examine your role in the demise of a relationship. This is an exercise in self-awareness, so direct your learning toward you. This is such an important thing to learn in life, especially if you are seeking more love. I've seen many people spend an inordinate amount of time trying to figure out what went wrong, and getting stuck when they concentrate on the other person's part in the breakup and neglect focusing on their own role.

Everyone has had at least one relationship that ended. Whether you are fifteen or fifty, whether you are a loner, a social butterfly, or somewhere in between, there was a time when you had a relationship with someone and it ended. Perhaps it was not an intimate involvement but a friendship or a business connection. That's not important. What matters is your role, what you did or didn't do, said or didn't say that contributed to the end of this liaison.

This exercise is not about blame but about responsibility. It is recognizing that you freely chose to get involved with this person, and that once you did, a combination of many forces contributed at first to maintaining the relationship and eventually to ending it. What was your role?

Did you change? Did he or she change? How did you react? Was the relationship less than honest from the beginning, and did things end when you became more frank?

Were there things about this person that you really didn't like and merely tolerated for a while? Did you decide one day you didn't want to endure them any longer? Had you given up on the relationship but let the other person make the break?

These are the questions you need to ask yourself. If you learn how to take responsibility for your part in a relationship, especially when it ends, you take a giant leap toward ensuring that you will not make the same mistakes again—even if you only learn not to get involved with the same sort of person. Acknowledge your part. See what role you played. A relationship, even the most casual one, is not a one-person affair. If you examine your role, you learn that your life is your creation. You are not a victim of circumstances. You create them.

Day three See work and play as one and the same. Allow no separation between the two. What you do as work is also play, and vice versa. However you make your living, whether you are a surgeon, a truck driver, or a musician, see your job as a game, as a playful activity that you would do even if you were not being paid to do it.

If you don't feel this way about your job, concentrate

on the smallest units of your work. Someone who works as a salesperson in a store does lots of little things. He dresses to play a part, asks people if he can help them, puts merchandise in order, makes casual chitchat with customers, answers questions, gets to trade clothes for money, works a cash register, writes out a receipt. Any and all of these activities can be seen as productive as well as playful.

Whatever you do, whether you use your hands, talk on the telephone, write, arrange things in a beautiful way, or take apart machines, a child does the same types of things. The only difference is that the child knows that what he's doing is play. To him, it's fun, and it's exactly what he wants to be doing from moment to moment.

The difference between work and play is an attitude, a thin line that exists only in your mind. Cross over frequently. Obliterate the distinction, and the heaviness of work can be replaced with the lightness of play for long stretches of time.

Day four   Listen to music that makes you think about love. It could be anything—rock, classical, jazz, opera, easy listening, New Age. Whatever it is, see if you can spend as much time as you can today immersing yourself in sounds that put you in a loving mood, that conjure up images of warmth and romance, of lovemaking, of feeling good about yourself, of being playful.

You can listen to tapes or the radio in your car, or lie back in the comfort of your own living room or bedroom. Of course, if there is someone special in your life with whom you can share musical tastes, and with whom you want to pass the time, by all means invite him or her to listen and play along with you.

For some, and I count myself among them, the deep, dark, emotional quality of opera inspires a loving mood, the feeling that my heart is open to the universe. For others, it may be the hard-driving beat of rock music. Or you may prefer the cool, urban sound of jazz, suggesting a wide range of feeling within the endless possibilities of city life. Or your sound may be bluegrass or country-and-western, music in which themes of loving, leaving, and forgiveness are often weaved into the songs.

If you listen to music—often—that makes you think of love, you too will eventually submit to its power. If you don't have a particular song or kind of music that moves you, ask a friend for a recommendation. Make a connection. This could be the start of something big.

Day five Develop a sense of what you find beautiful in people. Since beauty truly is in the eye of the beholder, begin by thinking about images or feelings you find exquisite. What are they? Is the look in your child's or lover's eyes when she's thinking beautiful? Does a piece of music compel you to think about harmonious things whenever you hear it? What constitutes beauty for you? Are you drawn by the particular form of a work of art?

What about faces? Whose face are you attracted to? How many faces do you see, either in person or in the media, that you consider to be truly perfect? What makes them so? Try to note the difference between inner and outer beauty. Think of a famous "beautiful person." Is this person also exquisite on the inside? Is he or she kind and considerate, willing to listen and pay attention? Or is he self-centered and rude, unaware of the effect he's having on you and other people? Is there any connection between inner and outer beauty? Which is more important to you? Have you ever met someone you didn't notice at first but came to find extremely compelling? Or vice versa?

Every age has a different concept of beauty. At certain times, plump, curvaceous women have been considered beautiful. In other times, like ours, thin, athletic-looking women are the standard of perfection. During the Renaissance, the Mona Lisa was considered a real looker. And in Colonial times, the size of men's calves was a measure of attractiveness.

How important is it to you to be around beautiful things? Can you create them yourself, perhaps with your words or deeds? Do you need to buy beauty, or can you see it all around you, in everyday possibilities and occurrences?

Day six   Go on an adventure. Make sure you are doing something you wouldn't normally do. Your adventure does not have to involve any risk, although without at least some emotional risk, it probably isn't much of an adventure.

If you have to plan ahead, by all means start now. Tell your boss or your assistant at work that you will be out for a day or a week as you commit yourself to this voyage of discovery. Your adventure may be a sailing trip on a lake or bay near your home, or your first massage, or a long car ride to visit your daughter unexpectedly at college, or an experimental weekend of love, sex, and intimacy. Find out as much as you can about what to expect before your adventure begins, but keep in mind that the unexpected parts of your voyage will emerge when you push your emotional envelope the most.

Bear in mind also that what is commonplace for someone else might be an adventure for you, and vice versa. On a trip to the Middle East with my parents years ago, I persuaded them to walk down a very narrow alley between two boulevards in Cairo. They were at first reluctant, but then they relented. We saw Cairo life as it is lived by residents, and it was fascinating to witness this. For me, the little side trip was interesting, but for my parents it was an adventure, an experience that took them out of their comfort zone. They still talk about it with enthusiasm and incredulity. Of course, you don't have to travel abroad to have an adventure. Deciding to replant your garden with vegetables, flowers, and fruit trees can be an adventure. Changing your career from investment banking to publishing can be an adventure, or getting involved with someone can certainly be an adventure.

The essence of an adventure is that you don't know what's going to happen, but you know you will be changed. Feel the excitement as you begin to plan and follow through on your excursion into the recesses of yourself.

$\mathcal{D}$ay seven Have a conversation with the president, or someone in high position. It doesn't have to be the current president. You can bring back Andrew Jackson or Franklin Roosevelt if you desire, but choosing the current president makes the most sense, because he is someone who can accept your advice or counsel and make changes.

Of course your conversation is imaginary. You can write letters to the president, but it's not as much fun as driving in your car and imagining that he or she is sitting next to you. You have his ear and you can talk about whatever you want to. What would you tell him? Everyone has opinions about how to make things better in the country and the world. This is your chance. You are going to spend the next hour talking to him—and you can make up his answer as well.

Remember, you only have an hour, so you can't get into

the details of a particular policy, or review how a crisis began. You can only concentrate on solutions. What should he do to bolster the economy? Is the problem too much domestic spending, or foreign competition? What about individual rights? How could he make opportunity truly equal? How about education? Health care? The rise of nationalism around the world? Is that a problem for us, or is this development none of our business? The president has your ear, and now is your chance to advise him on how to proceed with your plans.

The ability to love is the ability to play with possibilities, and having an imaginary conversation with someone in a position of political power is a good way to explore complex topics lovingly.

Day eight   Indulge in nostalgia. Spend the day thinking about the past, how splendid it was, how much simpler life used to be, when traffic was lighter, the sky bluer, the subway trains cleaner, when you could stay out until dark exploring the neighborhood without thinking about your safety. Allow yourself the luxury of remembering everything at its best, and see if you can conjure up the details that will make your memories vital. If you don't have great memories, fantasize about how it could have been.

Pull out your photo album, old movies, or letters from friends or family members to help catalyze your trip back into time. You can use this opportunity to tell your children or grandchildren all about living during the Second World War, or growing up in the fifties, when many families seemed to come out of Norman Rockwell paintings, or the sixties, when Motown and go-go boots were hot stuff. Recall the clothes, the music, the sayings, the radio or television shows, the movie stars. Tell your son or daughter about the automobiles, what it was like to drive a '53 Chevy Belair with two-tone colors and crushed velvet seats, and a steering wheel the size of a manhole cover.

Allow yourself to remember the olden days with fondness and affection. Think about how friendly and helpful people were, how easy it was to talk to your neighbors or start a conversation with a stranger. Recall what it was like to say "neat," or "groovy," or "daddio," like Maynard G. Krebs in the sitcom *The Many Loves of Dobie Gillis*, a hit television show in the late fifties and early sixties.

When you indulge in nostalgia, you satisfy a longing we probably all have, a desire to relive moments that made us feel good. Nostalgia is, of course, only part of the story. We usually edit out our memories of what was scary, unfair, or difficult about a past time. Nostalgia demonstrates your preference for interpreting your life in a positive manner, for seeing the good, for remembering fondly, and this helps you to live well in the present. See if you can, from this day forward, create memories of your loved ones that will last a lifetime.

Day nine   Daydream. Take the time today to let your mind wander wherever it wants to go, whether that is a certain place or a specific time, or a combination of both. Allow yourself the luxury of entering a dreamlike state during waking hours, without any objective other than the sheer pleasure of relaxing your mind.

You can set aside a designated time for daydreaming, take a walk in a serene location where there are no cars and few people, or just daydream as you move about during your regular day. The choice is yours. If you find daydreaming hard at first, stay with it. Before long you will find your mind wandering to far-off places, conjuring up images that arise from the innermost part of you, the part that houses your true nature.

When you daydream, what do you think about? Do you project yourself into the future, seeing yourself in particular surroundings with familiar people accompanying you, or do you find yourself going back to the past, remembering a particularly loving or beautiful time in your life? How does this make you feel?

Try to daydream every day, even if it's for a few minutes between responsibilities. Keep in mind that your ability to love includes the ability to follow your subconscious. Daydreaming will help you do this. Daydreams are not irrelevant or insignificant moments. The seeds for future developments in your life are contained in the things you imagine.

Day ten   Make things fit. See how many different ways you can put objects together that seem to belong with one another, spatially or chronologically, or in more human ways—physically, emotionally, mentally. This is obviously something that has no apparent purpose, but it is playful and also can be very instructive. Love is about disparate parts fitting together. If you see how tangible objects can be united, you will see how intangible qualities can too.

Do a puzzle. It doesn't have to be a large one. Any size will do. Spend some time thinking about the pieces and how you can make them match. When you find a piece that fits and you put it in its place, how does it feel? Does it provide you with satisfaction when that piece you've been searching for is inserted neatly into its proper slot?

Wear clothes that fit you very well. Reject any article that isn't your exact size, even if you like the color or style. You can also be ambitious and rearrange cabinets or shelves in your closet, pantry, or refrigerator. Or take on your desk at home or at work. Take everything out, throw away what you don't want, and put things back in perfect order, even if this new arrangement lasts only a day.

What about people? Who goes with whom? You can play matchmaker and put together two single friends, or just arrange for two people who might enjoy knowing each other to meet. Perhaps you know of a part-time job that would be right for your neighbor's son.

Look for opportunities to match things up, to assemble

something so that it is whole and all the parts are in the right place. If you look around, and also think about the situations and people who are close at hand, you'll come up with a variety of opportunities to practice your skills.

Now, open your sock drawer and take out all the socks. Put aside the ones that have no partner and fold together the remaining ones. Do you see the connection between pairs and love?

Day eleven   Pick up a musical instrument. It really doesn't matter how proficient you are—whether you've never played one before or you've taken a few lessons. Just express yourself through the medium of the instrument. Allow the part of you that likes to play come out through the sounds of the instrument. If you absolutely have no musical ear, you can draw a picture with markers, crayons, colored pencils, or watercolors. The point of today is to express your creativity.

If you have access to a piano, sit down and string together a few notes. Even if your repertoire is limited to "Twinkle, Twinkle Little Star," start with that. Forget about what you have to do or where you have to be. Just let the minutes and maybe the hours pass while you bang out a few bars of music.

If you've never played any instrument before, it may be difficult to make the violin or clarinet sound palatable. Try the drums. You can rent a set of bongos for the day and work out some combinations with your hands, feeling the rhythm within you and making and expressing it through the stretched skins on wooden frames between your knees. Or pick up a xylophone or tambourine, put on some music you like to listen to, and play along with the band.

If you have decided to draw, you can create a pastoral scene or an abstract image or just let the combination of colors guide your activity. You can devote your effort to one composition or make a series of sketches.

The point is to engage your playful side, to channel your energy toward something artistic and fun, something we all have within that is often looking longingly for an opportunity to emerge. What about the harmonica, or the guitar you bought twenty years ago that is still sitting in your garage. Use your voice as an instrument. Experiment with tunes you never tried before, or stay with one song and sing it perfectly from beginning to end.

Playfulness is rather like entering a different state, a state that is within you but doesn't often get a chance to come out. See if you can let down your guard for just a little while and be the uninhibited star you always dreamed of being.

Day twelve   Write a love letter. This is not a serious letter but a playful one. This missive can be addressed to anyone, including yourself, and you don't even have to send it if you don't want to, although if you know you are not going to before you start out, then you might not give it your best effort.

This letter is an expression of what you love about life, what you find most pleasing, most satisfying, most enjoyable. It can take the form of a list, although it won't be as poetic if you merely write down the things you love without elaborating. You can address this letter to your partner or your kids, to a best friend, or, as I said, to yourself. If you choose the last course, make sure you mail the letter.

Be sure to include those things that really move you. If you have an adventurous spirit, write about your visits to exotic places and how you feel when you are faced with the challenge of learning strange customs and practicing a language that is not your native tongue. If you love family life, write about how great it feels to come home from work at the end of the day and sit down to a delicious meal with your wife and kids, indulgently discussing your respective days, looking at their bright eyes and smiling faces as they devour their plates of pasta.

If you love the fact that you are you, write about that. Elaborate on what you've gone through to be the person you are, the obstacles you've had to overcome, the challenges you've met. But also write about the people who have helped you, who've encouraged you, who recognized your talent when you were unsure, who made phone calls on your behalf and listened empathetically when times were tough.

Whatever you choose to write about, make sure the

glue that ties it all together is the reality of love, that you speak and write with feeling, that you know and express how much these circumstances or people mean to you. Make sure also that you are not afraid, embarrassed, or reluctant to express yourself. By telling the world what you love and writing about it from your heart, you know that you pave the way for these qualities to increase, and you affirm what you like and who you are by trumpeting the message for all the world to see.

If you make a regular habit of this, if you periodically write about what's important in your life, you are taking steps to ensure that these parts will flourish in whatever form life chooses to present them to you.

Day thirteen   Play with an idea. It can be one that you think of, one that a friend or your partner suggests to you, or one that you read about in a newspaper, book, or magazine. It might be more fun in fact to bring someone into your game, to discuss this idea with someone, so the two of you can see the idea from as many sides as possible.

You can play with an idea the same way you play with any tangible object. Just take up the idea and run with it, as if it were a football and you were sprinting to the goal line. Let's say your notion is packing up your entire life and moving to London. You have no contacts there, no idea at this time what you're going to do when you arrive, how long you are going to stay, where you are going to live, and whether or not you will even like being there. You may or may not have ever visited London before. That doesn't matter. Just play with the idea of going. You may never go, but that's beside the point as well. What counts is that you think about living in London from every conceivable angle, taking every possible factor into consideration. You make your idea become real as you play with it.

If the idea involves your family, get them involved in the discussion. Ask your partner and kids or your parents and siblings what they think of your idea. Write down some of the questions involved in such a move. What about your jobs? How will you live when you get there? Why would you want to do this in the first place? Is London the city you really want to move to, or is it really Paris? What about school? Is that a consideration in your deliberations?

When your playing session is over, see how you feel. Are you energized or drained? Do you have a clear image of where you're going with your idea, or are you holding back from really letting your creativity take over?

Day fourteen Watch a sporting event. You can choose a match that is televised, make plans to attend a baseball or football game, or visit a local park and watch two people play tennis. And if you live in a city or town that has a large ethnic population, chances are there will be a soccer match going on someplace nearby, or even a game of bocce if you live near an Italian community. Whatever the game or nature of the competition, watch the event as a spectator.

See how the competition develops, which people perform which roles. See how the coaches direct their respective teams if you're watching a group sport, or how the individual players handle themselves if you have chosen to view one-on-one competition. Why do fit bodies in motion hold people's attention? What can you learn from watching athletes perform, whether it's at the highest level of competition, where young men and women earn millions of dollars per year playing baseball, basketball, or golf, or at the level of Little League or a neighborhood football game?

If you're watching professional players, either in your own living room or at the contest itself, watch what they do when they're not playing. How does an infielder relax between pitches? Do individual players have different rituals they perform? What is the difference in skill between this level and high school? How do some players get to the professional level? Are they born with more talent, or do they practice incessantly out of a great desire to reach the professional ranks?

Look for great plays. See what makes you respond or what gets the crowd cheering. Try not to care who wins. Try to let go of rooting for one side, and see if you can appreciate the caliber of the play, how someone can hit a drive just to the end of the tennis court, or how a person can stand over a tiny golf ball and stroke it to within a few feet of the hole.

What is the attraction of sports? Is it the entertainment aspect, the competition, or the excitement of seeing people perform at a level beyond the reach of other players? What can you learn from this? How can it change your idea of life and love? Is there something to be gleaned about being fully engaged—in body, mind, and spirit?

Day fifteen   Learn how to lose. Since you've spent some time watching a sports event, think about the nature of losing. See if you can remember times when you've competed, whether in athletic or gambling situations, for a job among many contestants, or for a boyfriend or girlfriend. If you're like most people, you've probably lost at various times, perhaps at cards or a board game, or hopscotch or any other childhood game. How did it feel? How did you take losing?

What does it mean to lose, anyway? What have you lost? Many people have difficulty learning, and therefore loving, because they don't know how to lose. They take losing personally, as if they were the only ones ever to experience this phenomenon. People who compete lose; there's no getting around it, and if you want to push yourself in any area of life, you'll probably face defeat at one point or another. Learn how to lose and feel successful anyway. Focus on the effort you've made, on the fact that you tried your best, that you did whatever you could to succeed.

At some point, you have to give up thinking about the reward. What matters is the attempt, the intensity with which you throw yourself into the fray, calling upon whatever resources you have—and keeping your integrity intact—to obtain what you desire. Let go of thinking about the outcome. If you try enough times, you'll succeed at something. Thomas Edison said that he had to invent the lightbulb because he had failed at everything else he tried.

If you learn how to lose, you will understand the nature of love, which is to make an attempt, to take risks, to be vulnerable, to get messy emotionally, to involve your entire being in the effort and feel great about it regardless of the outcome. I remember, as a young man in my twenties, infatuated again, telling my best friend of my latest heart-throb. He asked if my feelings were reciprocated, to which I replied that I wasn't sure. He said, "Win or lose, you win." I've never forgotten that. In that case, I lost; but really, I won. Why? Because I had loved, and my success was in experiencing the feeling, not whether it was requited.

Day sixteen   Spend the day soliciting suggestions from others. Forget about what you know, or think you know, and be receptive to others' wisdom. Having more love in your life means being open to the experience of others, and one way you can benefit from that experience is through suggestions.

You can choose to be open about things that are important—like job or career choices, or matters of the heart—or you can solicit suggestions about a great novel or biography to read, where to go for the weekend, or what you should do to change your appearance. You can ask for advice from people who are close to you, like your family members, a friend, or your partner, or you can range much further afield, to business associates, colleagues, or acquaintances. If you take public transportation to work, you can engage in a conversation with the person sitting next to you, and if you are adept at this, before long you will feel free to ask him or her, "Say, where can I find the best burrito in town?" Who knows, she might have an opinion.

So often, we miss great opportunities to learn something new because we think we know everything and never bother to ask. To me, it's the ultimate in arrogance. It's the quickest route to leading a lonely life, to closing yourself off to the ideas and suggestions of other people. I'm not talking about your aunt Mabel, who can't stop telling you how to dress even though her preference in clothes is not what you would consider tasteful. I'm talking about the courage to ask for help, to understand your limitations, to know when you don't know something, or to know that someone else, whose opinion you trust, might help you contribute to a better understanding of an issue.

Day seventeen Practice something. Whatever it is you want to accomplish, or improve upon, work at it. You're going to set up a schedule and stick to it, so make sure it's one you can handle. Don't make it so burdensome that you give up easily when you find you have been unrealistic about the amount of time you could spend on this, but also don't make it so easy that you don't challenge yourself. Make sure it feels right to you.

What skill do you want to practice? Do you want to improve your massage technique? Learn to play the violin? Speak Spanish? Do you want to act? Become a writer? Practice. If you want to take a course or get a coach or tutor, that's fine, too, but the greatest advances in your skill level will come from your own efforts.

It's better to spend several minutes daily than a lot of time infrequently. One hour a day for a week is better than seven hours one day. Set aside the time. Forget about instant results. You may have them, commonly called beginner's luck, but sooner or later you will probably reach a plateau that you can only surmount through steady practice. Don't look for shortcuts and easy answers. They will come to you when you're ready for them, and that too comes from practice.

Some years ago I wanted to become a better swimmer. I began to practice regularly and learned a few techniques, and after noticing some improvement, I started to think that I was beginning to reach the upper limit of my ability to move through the water smoothly. I kept at it and then one day in the pool I felt like a fish, swimming gracefully and with ease.

Practice is the activity that engages your whole being. It gathers together all your faculties and creates a new you.

Day eighteen   Explore a myth. See whether it affects a deep, inner part of you, or helps you to understand life better. Why are myths a part of our culture?

Myths are a way in which a culture seeks to understand the most basic, most human qualities. They are also a way to explain difficulty, to capture in story form the complexities and contradications that characterize our attitudes and behavior. Myths teach us that we are not alone, that others may have felt the way we do.

There are a number of myths you can explore. One of the most famous to come out of the Middle Ages was the myth of Tristan and Iseult, the myth of ultimate romantic love. Find out why this tale inspired songs and stories and sparked a sea change in the way in which Western civilization saw love, and why troubadours began to roam the countryside of southern France singing ballads of fair maidens and knights who idolized them. What does this myth tell us about our culture, and also our psyches?

Or you can choose an ancient Greek myth. The Greeks developed myths to understand the varieties of human behavior through stories of the actions of gods and goddesses. Do you know the myth of Atlas, a giant who was compelled by Zeus to carry the heavens forever on his shoulders? Or the myth of Sisyphus, who was forced to roll a huge stone up a hill, only to endure the repeated frustration of having the rock fall back down as he neared the summit?

What are the lessons of the myth? What do we human

beings need to learn about life? About love? About our enduring condition? How can you understand your experience more deeply through the symbolism of fables and fairy tales? What is there in our makeup that enables us to understand enduring principles when they are told through someone else's experience?

What is your favorite myth? Do you have your own personal myths, about you or your culture? Explore a myth from our culture—the myth of Horatio Alger, for example. What does this myth tell you about success, about our democracy or the free-enterprise system? Do you believe the myth of rags to riches? Do the people around you?

Day nineteen   Visit a foreign country. Obviously, you have to plan such a trip unless you live near the northern or southern border of the United States and can easily slip into Canada or Mexico. But even if this is possible, make sure you go deep enough into one of those countries to really experience the native culture, not an Americanized version of it.

You can choose a country you've been to before, or one that you have not previously visited. If your budget does not allow a trip, act as if you are going anyway by getting as much material as you can from whatever sources you can. You can borrow books from the library or buy them in a bookstore, read magazines about your chosen country, or rent a movie or two that takes place in the land of your choice.

When you visit this country, do so with the idea that you are there to learn as well as to enjoy the sights and sounds. See if you can pick up enough of the language to go beyond the customary tourist spots to remote places. Eat in local restaurants. Visit sites that explain the history and culture. Explore the differences in attitudes, behavior, and values.

Perhaps your stay in a foreign country will enable you to know yourself better, to learn more about your own expectations, to see your own country or hometown in a different light. Feel the exhilaration of communicating in a foreign tongue. See if you can turn the country of your choice into a giant classroom, learning new things as you also enjoy the sights, smells, tastes, and feelings you experience when you are there. You'll know you are making great progress when you begin to dream in Italian, Japanese, or Turkish.

Day twenty   Surround yourself with people who make you laugh. Spend the day devoted to enjoying those who have the ability to poke fun at themselves, who don't take things so seriously, who can see the absurd side of life, the side that keeps reminding you that you're ultimately not in control of everything.

See if you can forget your troubles, aggravations, irritations, frustrations, and disappointments for a day as you get together with people who pledge to do the same. Devote yourself entirely to play and merriment. Go to or rent a movie that is guaranteed to make your stomach ache from laughter. Organize a game with your friends—like charades or Twister—that will fill your day with mirth. If your tastes run to the literary, act out a comedy by Shakespeare, like *A Midsummer Night's Dream* or *A Comedy of Errors*. Keep in mind that the point of all this is to laugh.

If you make laughter a priority in your life, you surely increase the chances of laughter finding you. But your environment is important. If you can spend the day with people who know how to have a good time, then your chances of going to bed tonight with a huge smile on your face increase a thousandfold.

Day twenty-one   Learn a new technique. It's not at all important what this is. It could be a new way of adding a kick to your cooking oil so that your food is spicier, but you don't have to bite into hot chili peppers. It could be a new dance step that pushes you to a higher level of proficiency in your drive to become the new Gene Kelly. It could be a better way to breathe while you are swimming, so that you're not wasting movement and getting unnecessarily tired. Or it could be learning how to make a conference call on your new telephone system at work. Whatever it is, be it a simple matter or something more complex, learn how to do it.

Learning is as much an emotional process as it is a matter of memorizing facts or paying attention to an instructor. If you are attentive to the process, learning a new technique will teach you everything you need to know about learning other things and you will become a lifelong learner. Even the simplest new skill can sometimes push the envelope of ideas you have about yourself.

No one can learn for you. You have to assume that at some point in your life you're going to be challenged to grow and all the learning techniques you ever developed will be brought to bear on the situation. How you learn to draw, speed-read, or lift weights is the same way you learn to deal with setback, heartache, or catastrophe. By learning to learn you are staying ahead of the changes that are inevitably taking place around you, at the same time that you develop parts of yourself you may never have known existed. You may even find that you have mechanical ability after all, that the only thing you needed was to give yourself the time to get the job done properly.

$\mathcal{D}$ay twenty-two Make a fool of yourself. Hold nothing back. Make this the purpose of your existence today. Do whatever it takes to make people notice you, to allow them to see your outrageous side. Play the role of the medieval court jester, whose task it was to entertain the ruler and his entourage with jokes and pranks and who got away with making fun of the king when no one else dared to.

In acting classes, one of the first exercises is to dramatize embarrassing things that would make you cringe if you saw other people doing them. You may have to emit animal sounds for fifteen minutes before the whole class, or make funny faces, or pretend you're a baby eating dinner. The point in acting is to strip away your ego, to realize that who you are is a construct you have created and that in order to play a role—any role—you have to be willing to do anything in front of other people. Well, today is your day to act, and your role is that of fool.

Ask your friends for suggestions. You might want to wear a bathing suit under your coat to a cocktail party, or volunteer to sing "Fly Me to the Moon" in front of your co-workers. Whatever you decide to do, just make sure that you are stepping outside your comfort zone, that you perform an act you feel uncomfortable doing. It might be as mild as wearing sparkly purple nail polish or a garter belt instead of panty hose, or something wild like walking up to a complete stranger you find attractive, inviting her to your cousin's wedding, and pretending that the two of you are secretly married.

Go ahead, be vulnerable. Risk your dignity and the image you have of yourself. See if you can survive the loss of the person you were yesterday, in favor of a much looser, much more adventurous you.

Day twenty-three Find out something about a great artist. It could be a painter, a musician, a writer, even a great leader. However you define art, learn something about someone you admire. Discover a characteristic about a man or woman who developed his or her skill to such a point that he or she is universally recognized as brilliant, or at least gives you pleasure.

Do you know much about Mozart or Beethoven? Did you know that Abraham Lincoln had a nervous breakdown as a young man, endured the death of his sweetheart, and lost numerous elections before he became president? Were you aware that Van Gogh never sold a single one of his paintings during his sad, troubled life?

What about Leonardo da Vinci? Are you familiar with the milieu in which he lived and worked? What can you find out about Renaissance Italy? What took place there that led to an explosion of creativity that we see embodied in Leonardo, who was an inventor as well as an artist? Do you know what it means to be a Renaissance person?

What about an artist of our own time? Whose work moves you? Do you have a favorite author? Is there a movie director or a comedian whose life would give you insight into your own? What was Katharine Hepburn's upbringing like? What were the influences that made Leonard Bernstein so talented in such a wide variety of musical forms? How could one person play a Mozart piano concerto so flawlessly and also compose the music to *West Side Story*?

Learning about a great and talented man or woman is also learning about yourself, because there are attributes that all human beings share. And when you know more about the life of this man or woman, you will also know more about love—the love she had for her work and the drive to develop her abilities. You'll also learn about the determination and persistence that carried her through difficult moments, about the way in which she bounced back from failure and disappointment, about the vision she had of herself that never faded from her imagination.

What can you learn from this person's life that helps you to understand your own?

The Pleasures of Work and Creative Self-Expression

I know a woman who boils her life down to three categories, and if these are all in alignment, life is grand: where you live, who you love, and what you do for a living. Well, by her standards, I've always given myself high marks in living and loving, but I must admit that until recent years I've had difficulty with the third.

I started college with the intention of becoming a lawyer, not because I wanted to be one but because I wanted to go into politics and the quickest route to political office was through law school. And of course I always had my mother in the back of my head, saying, "You're so smart, and you make everything sound right—be a lawyer."

Two things happened to me. I couldn't abide the pre-law courses, and I was completely turned on to the study of history by one of my professors, whose love of his subject was equaled only by his mastery of it. I had never had the pleasure of being in the company of someone who so obviously loved what he was doing. He inspired me, and I dropped all thoughts of law school, politics, and being a dutiful son and went on to get my

Ph.D. in history. It was my first lesson in self-expression—you have to love what you're doing in order to make it work for you, to feel successful, to derive satisfaction, even to earn money. These elements are all intertwined, and if you try to pull one out—monetary success, for instance—without paying attention to the others, the whole fabric unravels.

To continue my story, academia ultimately didn't suit me either, but at least now I had stepped off the path of *having to,* and had walked onto the path of *wanting to.* I had learned how to evaluate a career from the perspective of who I was, rather than simply what I wanted to earn. As my career developed, I recognized that the jobs I took and the situations I chose were ones that taught me to be the person I was destined to become. I learned how to write for popular consumption rather than for academics, how to communicate to a broad audience through years in sales and marketing, how to supervise people and manage projects as an executive, how to raise funds, plan strategically, and master corporate finance.

As soon as I recognized what my professional life was all about—that through these many incarnations I was learning skills that were making me into a complete person, that I was developing abilities I never knew I had, that I was staying open to opportunities—the frustration of not finding the right work became tolerable, and I could bear whatever pain or discomfort I was experiencing because I knew these trials and tribulations were growing pains.

I am now reaping the benefits of the hard work and the difficult lessons I needed to learn over the years. I have never felt more fulfilled in what I do. I am my own boss, write books, counsel people and lead seminars on love, relationship, and personal fulfillment issues, and introduce total strangers to each other, who sometimes become true partners. I love my work, and because of this, my relationships with my family, friends, and everything else are affected in a positive way.

Some very fortunate people are passionate about what they do, whether they put together computer systems, give massages, or teach young children how to read. We lucky ones are "in love" as much as any lover is. We have learned to devote ourselves to a calling and derive pleasure from that devotion in the rewards that come from mastery of our subject or profession. This love is no different from love for another person. It's no longer work if you love it. It's love. You can call it whatever you want—your passion, creative self-expression, right livelihood—but if it's appropriate it will contain the same elements as love with another person does: focus, reverence, care, consideration, time, and attention.

Success in life and success in work come from the same source, from a desire to connect fully with a part of yourself. If you are truly successful in the work world, you are more likely to feel this positive energy penetrate the rest of your life, including your love life.

Day one Delegate with trust and clarity. Commit yourself to the idea that you are capable of clearly communicating to someone else exactly what you want done, that he or she is fully capable of executing it, and that letting go of having to perform every aspect of a project is safe and comfortable for you.

Make sure you see the entirety of what you want to do, so that you know how every part fits into the whole. If you are launching a publicity campaign for a major new product, assign the tasks of writing the press release, sending it to the media, following up on the correspondence, and doing the interviews, and make these tasks fit the skills and abilities of the human resources at hand. Make sure each participant understands the whole project, what the objectives are, and how the successful execution of each task will realize the goals.

The ability to delegate is one of the most critical—and underrated—management skills. People who hover over every detail of their work are narrowing their scope of potential success. Those who can delegate wisely, with patience and understanding, are usually those who have performed the delegated tasks themselves. They know how long something might take and what the potential difficulties and frustrations are. They also know that no one of us is as smart or productive as all of us working together.

Day two   Praise your boss. If you have a supervisor, let him know how much you appreciate his skills, how patient and understanding he is, how much you've learned from his tutelage. Very few people understand the concept of managing a boss, but the ones who do understand it know how important it is in fashioning and maintaining a successful work experience.

The work world can be a threatening place, which is why praise and support are so important. People may let a teacher know how inspiring and brilliant she is but feel reluctant to praise a boss, as if being on top reduces the need for approval. I learned this important step with great difficulty, usually when it was far too late to repair relationships that had begun to fray. I was under the mistaken impression that my bosses had to be perfect people, know everything, in short, *deserve* to be my superiors. It wasn't until I became a boss myself that I realized how fragile and tentative the position of supervisor is, how uncertain and frightening things often are. When I reflect on my troubled relationships with bosses, I realize now that I needed to have more compassion.

You can find much to praise in your boss—her vision, office political skills, support and encouragement, willingness to take risks, dedication and hard work, and clever ability to make good decisions, including hiring you. It's so much easier to develop a productive, respectful relationship with someone when she feels she's earned your appreciation, even if you are giving her the benefit of the doubt. It's certainly not necessary for someone to be perfect to be a good boss, just as it's not necessary for your son, daughter, husband, or best friend to be perfect for you to love him or her. It's a matter of looking for the good and accentuating it, rather than looking for the fly in the ointment and judging the entire tube.

Day three Set a positive example at work. Act in such a way that other people seek to emulate you, not because you do everything right and rigidly maintain a standard with which no one can compete, but because you are balanced and centered and because your work reflects an authenticity that everyone around you—your co-workers, colleagues, supervisors, and employees—can readily see and be inspired by.

Maintain a "can-do" attitude. Let other people talk about what hasn't been done, can't be done, or won't be done. Talk about what can be done, has been done, and will be done. Go about your work with quiet confidence, making steady progress without frenetic fanfare or quiet desperation. Talk openly about any problems with the people who need to hear about them, without rancor, hostility, or arrogance. Your byword should be cooperation, and everything you think, say, or do should be directed toward this end.

Be a mediator and reconciler. Be a person who always

makes an effort to move things forward, who lets others express their frustrations and instead looks for a positive interpretation of events. Be available for people. Let them know with subtlety that you have the ability to see all sides, that your judgment is sound and fair, and that you are willing to take a chance on someone else's ideas. Regardless of your position in your company and of whether you are one of ten, twenty, or a hundred thousand, act in accordance with your nobler parts.

Day four   Neutralize your feelings about money. Give up trying to understand it as a material thing, as something thought of in terms of more and less, wealth and want, rich and poor. See it rather as a fundamental element that enables your life to flow freely, a vehicle for doing what you want to do, having those things that bring you joy, experiencing those moments that empower you.

See money as energy. Elevate other forms of riches—friendship, intimate love, a good reputation, kindness, and gentility—to the status of your desire to earn more and more money. If you haven't placed enough importance on money, if you are always in debt, if your appetites far outpace your resources, if you constantly live off the energy of others, then it's time to elevate money's place in your life, to create more energy yourself so that you are free to focus less on obtaining cash and more on the direction and quality of your life.

If you transform your concept of money from something concrete to something more fundamental—like energy— you're likely to make better choices about it. You can relate to money the way you relate to food. You take in as much nourishment as you need to have energy for a specific period of time. Food and money are similar. You require a certain amount of it to survive and prosper, but after a point you must think of other ways to utilize this energy or it can weigh you down. If you have a more balanced attitude, one that will not hinder your quest for self-expression, you'll find that you will end up with the right amount of money.

Day five Create a collegial atmosphere at your office. This can take many forms, from organizing a weekly company softball game or bowling league, to getting together at the end of the day on a regular basis to have a drink and talk in a relaxed way about what's going on in your lives.

I have many fond memories of this type of activity. In the mid-1980s my co-workers and I got together every Friday after work at a local hangout for beer and hors d'oeuvres. As the executive director of this organization, which published materials on world hunger and which had undergone quite a bit of turmoil prior to my arrival, I wanted to encourage a cooperative spirit among employees. I made it easier for people to attend these soirees by having the organization pay each week for the first $20 worth of beverages. Our weekly gatherings were successful beyond anyone's imagination. Although not everyone always attended, we all knew that it would be an opportunity to connect with fellow employees away from the pressures of the office, and the camaraderie was very satisfying. Even the founders of the organization were often present.

In another work situation, the custom was to take someone out to lunch on his or her birthday. If your staff is large enough, you'll get to go out at least once a month. Or you can plan to have small parties at your and your co-workers' homes. A simple get-together with music and snacks will do the job of fostering an attitude of togetherness and support.

Day six Write down your fears about your work. Make a list of all the things you think are holding you back from being more successful, or are preventing you from feeling better about what you do—for a living, as a volunteer, or whatever. Next, write down the things you fear most about your work situation, or about another situation you may be contemplating.

It could be anything. You could fear making a change that you feel in your gut is right, but might entail a short-term reduction in your pay. Or you may be fearful of making a change even though you'd be getting a substantial raise, because you're afraid of the independence and responsibility this position entails. You may simply be afraid of losing your job, fearful of the future and its uncertainty. Write this all down.

When you identify and make explicit your fears, you clarify exactly what is holding you back from making a change, and you also begin the process of eradicating those fears. Fears rarely go away on their own. They disappear when you look at them. Fears don't like light. They thrive in darkness. Don't give them a breeding ground. Expose them, either to yourself or to someone close to you. Bring them to consciousness—and then release them. You can cross them out and replace them with affirmations. For instance, you can cross out "I'm terrified of losing my job even though I dread going in every day," and write instead, "I am bright and capable and am in a situation that reflects my passion and commitment." Or you can burn or bury the piece of paper. The important thing is to let your fears go symbolically and replace them with something positive and inspiring.

Getting more love out of what you do involves eliminating the fear of moving ahead, of the future. It means having faith that you and your professional destiny are looking for each other and that you will take whatever steps are necessary for the two of you to meet, including letting go of the barriers that prevent a good connection. It's like any relationship you have. If you bring your baggage with you, it burdens the contact from the start. Empty your bags. Let go of your fears.

$\mathcal{D}ay\ seven$ Have a muse. Develop a sign, symbol, or token that enables and encourages you to be creative, to do your best at work, to help you through difficult or uncertain situations. It may be the occasional presence of your cat, or a small gift that was given to you by a special person and remains sentimentally valuable. Whatever it is, have it close by, and let it become your guiding light, the path down which you move whenever you feel the need to be creative or receive help.

Are you involved in delicate negotiations for a new contract or lease? Are you dreaming about a promotion? Do you want to write more fanciful cover letters? Invoke your muse.

The idea of the muse comes from Greek mythology. The Greeks felt that creativity was inspired by an external force that supplied the individual with the means to go forward creatively. If the muse was present, the impulse to create would also be present. If the muse was not to be found, then the person was incapable of creation.

What could your muse be? Bring in a cute picture of your partner or kids and put it on your desk at the office. Carry something with you, a chain, locket, or shell you brought back from vacation many years ago, and look at it when you want to be inspired, when you need to ask for help from the powerful creative forces outside you.

Muses can also change. They don't need to stay the same. My muse at this particular time is morning sunshine.

Dreary days, days overcast with clouds or fog, and intense afternoon heat and light do not move me. I'd much rather turn inward and conserve my energy during this time, gaining strength for the creative work of the next day.

If you have a muse, you're not alone. You are invoking powerful, universal forces to help guide you and encourage you to do your best.

Day eight   Acknowledge your success in the moment. Regardless of your ambition, of where you want to be next year, or where you were the year before, look at where you are right now, in the present, and see it as a success.

Success is not about the glories of the past, or the dreams of the future, although these are not unimportant. Success is right now. What is going on in your life about which you feel terrific? Are your kids doing well in school? Are they happy, healthy, and well adjusted? Acknowledge that. Although they are obviously independent and ultimately responsible for themselves, you had a hand in their development. Appreciate your work, patience, and dedication.

What about your home? Do you enjoy your house or apartment? Do you just love being where you are? Make note of that, and thank life for your good fortune. Do you love your work? Acknowledge that. Do you love elements of your work, even though some of it could be improved? Notice what works.

In order to think of yourself as successful, to feel one with success, you have to generate the feeling from within. And that comes from looking at your life and seeing what works. Complaining about what doesn't work is not the way to future success. If you want to indulge in complaining as a spur to action, by all means allow yourself the luxury. But be quick about it and move on to a more positive attitude.

Success breeds success. Talk positively to yourself. The glass is always half full, regardless of whether certain things are not to your liking. If they're not, change them by focusing on what is working. If you look hard enough, you'll find more successful parts of your life than you expect.

Day nine Be disciplined about something. Decide to do a project, either at work or at home, with or without a friend, and stick to it over time. You could decide to make a life change, like becoming a vegetarian, giving up all animal flesh. Or you could decide to stop complaining about how bad things are, how rude people have become, how much life disappoints you, and discipline yourself to be more positive, to see the bright side, to look at the silver lining and not the cloud.

First, you have to make a personal commitment to your

discipline. You have to decide that this is really what you want to do. Forget about halfhearted attempts or lukewarm resolve. Your discipline might be something you've been thinking about for a long time, like taking up the guitar once again after a seventeen-year hiatus, or giving up caffeine or cigarettes. Write down your goal. Make it simple: "I am replacing cigarettes with exercise, better breathing, and a lot of laughter," or "I am making sixty cold calls per week at my new sales position." Carry your affirmation around with you. Refer to it often. If it inspires you, it can become your muse.

Be realistic about your discipline. You don't have to run every day to be a devoted runner. You can choose to exercise every other day, or even twice a week. Only do what you're capable of, but see if you can stretch it a bit, too. If you feel the urge to backslide, to give up, to let your discipline go, look at your affirmation. It will help you to keep your resolve. Think of your progress. Acknowledge how far you've come. Don't say to yourself, "My goodness, it's only been three weeks since I last took a cigarette, and I feel like having one now. How am I ever going to stop?" Instead, say, "Wow, it's been three whole weeks since I last took a puff, and I can breathe so much easier already. This is a breeze. I can do this."

If you want to nourish the part of you that derives love from your creativity, from your self-expression, you'll have to include discipline in your repertoire of skills. Remember what George Bernard Shaw said about success—it's ten percent inspiration and ninety percent perspiration.

Day ten   Think about the price you are willing to pay for success. You have to give up something for everything you want, whether it's a house in the country, a set of tools, or financial independence. So when you think about what you want to have, think about the price it costs you to get it.

Do you want to have more money than Midas? You definitely can have it. But are you prepared to forgo other pleasures in life for perhaps a long time to earn the money? Are you willing to put family life, intimate relationships, possibly your health, at least your emotional health, a distant second to work? Can you see yourself putting in twelve hours a day, every day, to make money? Can you afford to devote the energy to learning about cash management, taxes and insurance, investment strategies, and other aspects of financial planning? That's often the price you have to pay.

What about fame? Do you want to be recognized, like a movie star? Do you want the perks, the expensive cars, the designer clothes, the ability to be anywhere at any time, at least when you are not working? If so, are you prepared to have photographers in your face wherever you go? Can you give up casually going out to restaurants because people are constantly asking for your autograph or wanting to tell you how much they enjoy your music, and all you want to do is have a quiet dinner out with someone special? Can you afford this?

If you don't want the responsibilities or constraint of having steady work, and want to cobble together a living in order to have more time for yourself, are you willing to deal every day with the anxiety of not knowing where your next dollar is coming from, of consuming energy figuring out how not to spend, rather than on how to earn?

Every person pays the price for the life he or she leads. The price of the freedom of entrepreneurship is the uncertainty of where your venture will take you. The price of being an employee may be having a boss who tells you what to do and how to do it.

Whatever you want, you can have. In making this decision, it helps to know what price you have to pay for it.

Day eleven   Take a vacation. You don't have to wait for the summer months to do this. It's a gift you can give to yourself at any time of the year. This is in many ways the most enjoyable part of work, the part that lets you get away but with the knowledge that the work will still be there when you return.

Enjoy giving work up for a while and letting go completely of the obligation to be responsible, to fulfill your duties, to listen and pay close attention. The tension that can build up is palpable, and at times the only way to release it is to take time away from ringing telephones, endless meetings, ponderous deliberations about money, and stacks of mail.

If you have kids, either pack them up with you or ship them off to their aunt's or grandfather's house for a week. Don't use them as an excuse not to go away for a while. The open road awaits you. Of course you can elect to take a vacation by airplane. If that fits into your plans and budget, then by all means treat yourself.

There is an old Zen saying that sometimes absence is presence, as the windows are in a house. It's the same way with creative self-expression. Sometimes it's just necessary to be elsewhere. Take a vacation. Get away from the routine and live another part of you—the part that can relax and enjoy not doing as well as doing.

Day twelve   Learn your own work rhythm. There are an infinite number of ways to work. It's important to figure out the best way for you and to work that way. If you do, you will undoubtedly find yourself more productive and happier. You will have more love in your life because you will feel connected to your principal activity, which is your work or creative self-expression.

One way to understand your work rhythm is to try different ones. Are you a self-starter? Do you like to work independently? You might want to think about being in business for yourself, becoming an entrepreneur, or being a salesperson who may work for someone else but is on the road most of the time and makes his or her own schedule.

Do you like to work around other people? Then think about working for a large company, one with many branches or divisions, one that employs a multitude of different people in various capacities, many of whom you can get to know over a period of time.

Do you like repetition? Do you have an aversion to surprises in your work and prefer to know exactly what you're doing from one day to the next? Then think about a job like inputting data or being a telephone operator or handling sales for a mail-order company. Even though the information changes from call to call or entry to entry, what you do every day is basically the same, and you can comfortably settle into a routine and free yourself up for other things at other times.

There is a job or work situation for every different kind of person or personality. There are helping professions, careers that involve money, jobs that require you to be outdoors or to get dressed up every day. You can be around animals, plants, or rocks. You can work near the ocean, in the mountains, or on the fifty-second floor of a skyscraper. But first you have to figure out who you are, what you gravitate toward, what kinds of activities and situations "work" for you.

Day thirteen   Take care of little things. There are times in the life of every creative person, even those who aren't working but are trying to make ends meet without much income or focus, when what you absolutely have to do is deal with the small matters that enable the big ones to occur.

This might mean running errands, or going through your files to look for ideas that you may have filed months or even years ago and that may be useful now. It might mean cleaning off your desk to see what's under the mound of paper scraps that has accumulated over time. Or it might mean spending a day returning phone calls that have remained halfway down your "To Do" list for a month.

Every job creates myriad "little things" that must be done to make the whole project work. Some people delegate these tasks to secretaries, assistants, and associates and rarely do them themselves. That's fine, but sometimes it's better to do them personally, to see what a job is all about.

Every cook knows how to prepare food, to select, cut, chop, mix, and blend. He or she also knows how to clean up, wash, and put away. Every able carpenter knows how to buy and carry wood, keep his tools in good shape, organize a job, estimate the cost accurately, and read blueprints. At the end of the day, he also knows how to clean up, put away, and keep the job site safe. This is because the cook, the carpenter, the executive, the physician, and the consultant all know how to do the little things, and they do them as often as necessary to be successful at what they do.

Today, take the time to do the little things. Bring a machine in for service, maintenance, or repair. Empty the wastebaskets, water the plants, or wash the windows of your office. Little things are only little because we think of them that way and because they are simple to complete.

Day fourteen Try something. Try anything. This may seem like a simpleminded suggestion, but for many people it isn't. Do you expend a huge amount of effort convincing yourself that something you might want to accomplish can't be done, or isn't worth the effort, that what you have in mind won't work, or if it will, will require too much responsibility? Before long, you can talk yourself out of any challenge, big or small. But there is beauty in effort. All you have to do is try.

You can do what you want. Even a simple phone call to an old friend, or a potential client or lover, is something you can undertake. What's important today is the effort, the attempt. The task itself is irrelevant. It could be a significant beginning, or something small or trivial. It could be the start of a grand concept, like working on a major report or sculpture, or a simple project like washing your car. The objective today is to overcome your resistance and do something.

I often smile to myself when I hear someone say that he or she is not a "creative" person, as if creativity is something that one either has or doesn't have. Creativity resides in effort. It's having the courage to take one tentative baby step into the waters of the unknown. It's getting comfortable with what you can do, being honest with yourself about what you enjoy doing. It's facing rejection and temporary defeat, knowing that the lessons of failure are in many cases the most valuable ones—in life, in work, and in love. And in many cases, it's emerging triumphant after overcoming obstacles and setbacks, using hardship as the bricks and mortar of success.

But first you must try. Sometimes the effort will produce the desired outcome. Sometimes the results will be different from what you expected. But whatever happens, you will never be the same person again. You will understand how to reach, to strive, to feel your own power and ambition, and know that wherever you want to go is attainable simply because you have the courage to try.

Day fifteen   Plan a retreat. One of the most interesting ways to develop a better understanding of what you do and how you do it is to get away from your usual environment, even for a day, with your colleagues and co-workers, and talk about what's going on. Organize a retreat. Take off the power suits and ties, and black pumps and hose, and get an entirely different perspective on your work. If this idea seems far-fetched and impractical, hold on to it anyway. Keep suggesting it, and at the right time it will come to pass.

Make sure someone is in charge of securing the site and making the necessary arrangements. Also, one person might want to put together the agenda, and include lots of free discussion time, when you allow your feelings about your job—and not just the duties or the tasks—to emerge. I have seen seemingly trivial work-related adjustments, like not keeping a day-to-day record of hours, produce major increases in productivity and efficiency, simply because employees suddenly felt trusted.

If you're the boss, make sure you let the people who work for you know that everyone is on equal terms for the duration of the retreat. There are no corner offices away from the company building. Encourage input and involvement. For many, it will be difficult to open up at first, so have patience. Call on people. Solicit their thoughts and contributions. Make everyone feel that he or she is as much responsible for the enhancement of your group or the management of your company as you are. A good leader makes leaders out of his followers.

Make sure you write up and distribute notes of the discussions you hold. Solicit feedback on how it felt to be working away from work, to see what you do from a different perspective.

Winter

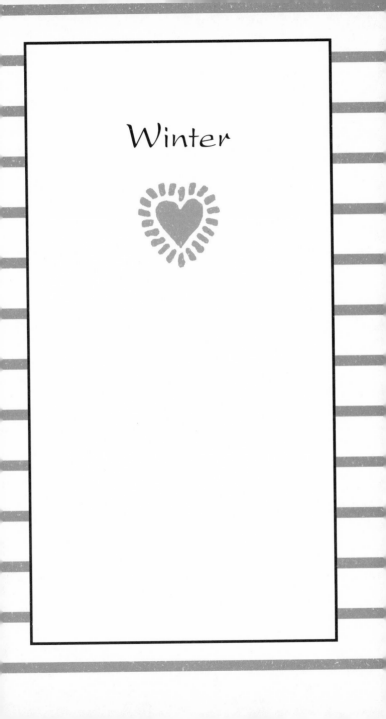

Family Lessons

Our relationship to both our family of origin and the families we have formed is the perfect practice ground for developing our ability to love in a deeper way. Although the connection between patterns learned in childhood and those repeated later as adults is evident, there are ways to relate to our families that can take us beyond blame, hurt, and guilt. The result can be more loving ways of living.

In my practice, interviewing hundreds of people seeking love, I find many of my clients think that if they had only come from different families they would be able to love easier, make surer choices, enjoy sex more, have higher self-esteem, and generally be a better person. But my sense is that in every family there are tendencies toward, and tendencies away from, love. Ultimately, your family is pretty much a given. You're not going to change your mother or your father, you can only influence your brothers and sisters by example, and you only have so much control over your children, possibly less than you think. So, as always, the focus comes back to the one thing you can change—yourself.

No family is perfect. Many people feel they come from dysfunctional families, but they often don't acknowledge the elements of their families that may nurture or support within the overall dysfunction. Again, I say you have a choice. You can either allow the fact that your family had or has problems to compromise your ability to love, or you can refuse to allow it. Even if your childhood was rooted in abuse, disease, alcoholism, abandonment, or sudden or premature death, you still have the choice, at any age, at any stage of your development, to love or not. And if you feel that you want to and never learned how, you have the choice to begin the process. There are people this very moment among your friends, family members, acquaintances, romantic partners, or colleagues, as well as a host of able professionals, who are willing to assist you. All you have to do is take the first step and reach out.

How you treat your family members—whether they are your kids, your siblings, your parents, or your in-laws—is your choice. How they treat or respond to you is at least somewhat dependent on how you respond to them. You can choose to relate to them with compassion and detachment, rather than take their behavior, if you don't like it, as a personal affront.

The only thing you really can do, and it's ultimately the greatest challenge, is to accept your family. I spent countless hours in my twenties futilely trying to convince my family members to live another way. But I've gotten over that. And now, in my mid-forties, I can't for the life of me figure out why I thought it was so crucial to argue and argue endlessly about political, personal, dietary, religious, and cultural matters with my mother and father. I see now that at the time I was only attempting to understand where my own life was going, or at least where I wanted it to go, and trying out ideas on them was a convenient way of testing my thinking. I thank my family members for their patience.

Families are what they are. Everyone absorbs some positive things and some negative things. Who is to say that you would have fared better in another situation? Perhaps you would now be more disciplined, but also more timid. Perhaps you would have more confidence, but would also be more reckless. Ultimately, if you are serious about loving yourself, you have to love everything about you, and that includes what you perceive to be both the light and dark sides. If you learn to accentuate the former, and to embrace and overcome the latter, then you will be more available to give and receive the love, attention, and affection both you and everyone around you desires and deserves.

Day one Organize a slumber party with your brother or sister. Invite a sibling you've been meaning to connect with, or one with whom you are particularly close, to spend the night. If you want to include another person, that's fine, too, but make sure your party is small enough to keep the interaction intimate.

If you want to try to arrange an out-of-town excursion, that would be ideal. To be away from your daily routine with your brother or sister will enable you to create much more closeness, without the obligations and expectations of everyday life.

Try to stay up as late as you can, doing activities you did as kids. Talk, play board or card games, listen to music, eat popcorn as you watch movies on television, read to one another, or share secrets. See if you can resurrect the feelings you had when you were younger, when summer vacation seemed to last forever, or when you looked forward to going to bed because it was an opportunity to check in and be close with each other, to discuss the ups and downs of your respective days.

What often prevents people, even people who are close family members, from connecting more deeply is lack of time. With our busy lives, it's now necessary to make time. Leave your kids and your spouses behind and take off with each other. You can put together an agenda beforehand or be completely spontaneous and let the evening evolve on its own. Whatever you choose, make sure you devote yourself to paying attention to each other, to sharing what's on your mind and in your heart, and to reaffirming your love and affection.

Day two   Accentuate the positive with your kids. Praise and acknowledge them, and tell them how much you love them, how wonderful they are. Spare no effort to let them know how important they are to you, how much you cherish and value them, even if you don't always see eye to eye on everything or if your relations are strained.

If you have small children, kiss and hug them frequently. Get as physically close as you can. Let them see by your actions how much you adore them, how attentive and willing you are to extend yourself to them. Don't wait for them to come to you, or "reward" them with your affection only if they're "good" and do what you tell them to do. Demonstrate your love for them today unconditionally, as if your feelings were a fountain that had no choice but to overflow.

If you have teenagers, they might not respond to such outpourings of physical affection, so you might have to be more subtle in your actions. Be specific. Remind them of things you like and value about them. Indicate over and over how much your sons or daughters mean to you, what wonderful people they have turned out to be. Again, regardless of the quality of your day-to-day relationship, make sure that today everything is all admiration, regard, and respect. If you think your child is a no-good, stubborn brat, then change your thinking. What you think is what you get, so start finding positive ways to view your child.

If you have no children, you can easily practice this suggestion with someone else's. Make sure you relate to your nieces, nephews, neighbor's kids, and godchildren in a positive manner. Perhaps you can even serve as a model for their own parents.

Keep in mind that your opinion of your kids and the way you demonstrate that opinion is probably the most important input in your child's life, whether he or she is seven, seventeen, or thirty-seven. You have tremendous influence on your child's self-esteem, and how much love both you and your child derive from your family has everything to do with how much of it you express. There is no greater, more significant place to show your feelings than with your kids. It's something you'll never regret, and you won't want to look back on your life when you are near the end and feel bad that you didn't let them know often enough how much they meant to you.

If you haven't demonstrated your best effort in this category, it's not too late to start. Many parents and children do not begin to have rewarding relationships until the child is well into adulthood. You can begin at any time.

Day three   Write a "love letter" to a parent. You can decide at the outset that your mother or father is not going to actually receive this letter, if that will free you up to express more fully what you want to say. Or you can go ahead and send it, deciding to do this before you write, or making the decision after you complete your project. The parent you choose to express your feelings for can be alive or dead, close by or far away, in or out of contact with you.

This love letter is different from ones you've perhaps written before, because it will reveal not only what you love about the parent but also what you don't particularly feel good about. The point is to express your feelings about this specific member of your family in a way that perhaps you cannot in person. Parents can be intimidating people, but the way to begin to reduce their impact on you is to express your feelings, and the way to begin to do that is to write to them as if you had every intention of sharing your outpouring with them, even if you don't.

Be honest and specific in your writing. If your father is generous but controlling, let him know how that makes you feel. If your mother allowed you to be independent but was never there for you, tell her that as well. Express your feelings rather than blaming her: "I felt so alone and abandoned when I was a child. I felt you really couldn't be there for me. I wanted your compassion when I encountered difficulties rather than feeling you resented my presence. I wanted your love and attention so much and felt I was just an extra burden. I know you had many children to care for, and now that I'm a parent I know how much energy it takes to be there in the way children require. It's not as easy as I used to think it was. I love you very much, and I would still like your undivided attention and care."

You can even start to deal with tragedies or crises if you haven't given yourself the opportunity to do that before. If you experienced physical or emotional abuse, alcoholism, divorce, or even suicide, you can begin the process of healing by releasing through words what you might have held on to for years.

Make sure you give yourself enough time to finish the letter. Try to do it in one sitting, so that you feel complete. You don't have to worry about grammar, spelling, or punctuation if you think they will slow you down. Just write from your heart and let your mother or father know how you feel about them. By expressing yourself in this manner, you will facilitate the opening of communication, even if your mother or father has passed on or is not in your life at the moment.

Day four   Interview and tape an older relative talking about his or her life. This works wonderfully with a grandparent or great-aunt or great-uncle, but it will also succeed with a parent, aunt, uncle, or cousin who is older than you.

Ask your relative to be expansive and especially attentive to detail. Think of the relationship between the two women in the movie *Fried Green Tomatoes*. You might want to jot down some questions before you begin, but make sure you address what life was like back when your relative was a small child. Are your assumptions correct? Were the twenties really "roaring"? What was the Depression like? World War II? If you're a teenager, you can find out all about the fifties and sixties and what your grandmother or uncle thought about hippies and acid rock music.

My maternal grandmother, who was born in 1885 and with whom we lived until I was thirteen years old, talked about the old days all the time. I really didn't have to interview her. She called her tales "stories," and by the time I was ten years old I knew all about her life before she came to America, who her relatives were, what they were like, and what village life was all about in Eastern Europe at the turn of the century. And now, thirty-five years later, I wish that what she recounted to me had been recorded.

You don't have to do the entire interview in one sitting. You can choose to concentrate on one topic each time you get together, or allow your relative to just go on about anything, asking questions for clarification. In this way, you will feel more connected to your family, to those people whose lives influenced the person you've become. You might even gain fresh insight into other family members, see them in a different light, understand them better. And perhaps you could turn your interviews into special gifts for all the relatives who are close to the person you interviewed.

Day five   Allow your kids to run the show. For one day, trade places and tell them that they are the parents and you are their children. They get to make all the decisions for the household. You can make requests, but the final choices are up to them.

If your six-year-old wants to go food shopping at 10:30 P.M., then get in the car and take off. If your toddler doesn't want to take a nap today, then she stays up because she is in charge. If your teenager wants to take $150 out of his savings account to buy a new bicycle, then that is his prerogative.

You might want to alert your kids when you're planning this day so they—and you—can be prepared for it. You have to go along with whatever they come up with as long as no one will be endangered by their suggestions. After all, skydiving might not be a great idea. But anything short of that is to be carried out with gusto and enthusiasm, just the way you like them to be on all other days.

Remember to be aware during the day of your inner protests and need for control, but try to keep these to yourself and act as if you are perfectly happy to watch Thomas the Train tapes all day, or spend hours transplanting flowers in your garden, or eat pizza for breakfast, lunch, and dinner. More important, how does it feel to give up control, to not be in charge, to feel what your kids must feel like most of the time? Do you like it, or does it make you anxious and uncomfortable?

Trading roles with someone close to you, especially a family member, is an unusual way of gaining a different perspective on your own life, one that will allow you to be more compassionate every day.

Day six   Discipline your kids in a positive manner. If you don't have kids of your own, you can practice this as an aunt, teacher, or friend. Or you may be planning to have kids someday. Start now to work on being able to define limits without threatening your kids' self-esteem.

First of all, tell them what you do want rather than what you don't want. Explain to your daughter that you would like her to brush her teeth and put on her pajamas before you read the bedtime story, rather than threatening not to read the story if she doesn't stop running around or being wild. Let her know firmly, clearly, and succinctly what you want and what the consequences will be if she ignores your request and wakes her baby brother. If you want her to get ready for bed, let her set the alarm or buzzer for five minutes. Give her that much time to complete the bedtime ritual. Kids love to make a game out of everything, so incorporate fun in the process.

Praise your children whenever possible. Tell them what great artists or helpers they are, how enchanting the garden looks since it's been worked on. If you have a small child and he or she still doesn't talk, act as if he understands every word you say. Chances are he absorbs more than you think, even if he can only communicate with grunts and other indecipherable sounds. Tell her how well she eats by herself, how wonderful she is at picking up things, how much you love her curiosity about the world. You can't praise enough. There is no danger of your kid getting a swelled head from too much praise. His entire life at this point is devoted to getting your approval, and the course of his future might be affected by how loving and supportive you are now.

Don't lose your temper. If at some point you want to stop negotiating with your four-year-old, just let her know that everything is no longer up for grabs. Try to leave some time for choices—even if it's between the red and the blue socks. Most parents run into difficulty with children because they are always rushing to be somewhere—gymnastics, swimming lessons, soccer practice. If your child's life is overextended, learn to simplify. This way, you won't be tempted to take it out on your child when you are frustrated at not having enough time in your life. You'll instead be patient and calmly direct about your requests.

Day seven   Tell your kids the truth. Even if your first impulse is to withhold information because you think the truth is too painful for them to hear, go ahead and say it anyway. You don't have to include all the gory details, but it's better for them to hear from you what's going on than to suspect or know the truth while you are still maintaining that everything is fine. If you don't have children, you might want to develop this awareness by learning to tell your parents the truth, or being candid with children who are not yours but are nevertheless close to you.

It doesn't matter how old the kids are—whether they are small children, teenagers, or adults with or without kids of their own—include them in your confidence. Let them know that their grandmother is ill and probably won't be with them much longer, or that there have been financial reversals in your family and you might be moving soon, or that you are having marital difficulties, and although you love them very much, you may be separating.

Kids are emotionally stronger than adults realize. Everyone at any age has an innate ability to process emotional information and handle it accordingly. Forget about "protecting" your kids from the harsh reality of the truth —what this often disguises is the real truth: that you want to protect yourself. And in doing so, you may hurt your kids by intimating that it is better to live in a "dream world" where everything is rosy, even though you—and they— know it isn't. If you can talk about money, sex, and death in a responsible, appropriate manner, you will be teaching your kids how to get along in life with more confidence and real knowledge about the world.

Withholding the truth from your kids may also create the fantasy in their minds that you are perfect, that nothing bad ever happens to you, and that you want them to think of you this way. Instead, be real. Let them know what's going on. Teach them by example that part of being human is to have foibles, faults, and difficulties, and that life includes problems that must be confronted.

I certainly do not mean to suggest that you should turn your child into your therapist. It is not healthy to burden him with your problems. What I am saying is kids know more than you suspect, and if you reveal the truth, you are helping a child mature and equipping him to face reality.

Day eight   Celebrate occasions with enthusiasm and delight. Create the kind of family life where events are observed consistently, where you and your kids can begin to look forward to birthdays, the winter holidays, or Mother's or Father's Day with anticipation, because everyone knows it's going to be special.

It doesn't matter what events or occasions you choose to celebrate, and you don't have to make a big deal about every one of them, although you might want to. Talk with your kids and other family members about this. If you want to go away for a summer holiday, decide to go on Memorial Day, Independence Day, or Labor Day, if you can't manage to go away on all of them. You can do the same thing every year or vary your activities. If you want to celebrate Mother's Day and you have three siblings, get together and agree to spend each year in a different home. Help build camaraderie by rotating responsibilities.

Children love celebrations, as do adults who still feel

like children from time to time. And if your family pays attention to these special times, you create wonderful memories that will stay with you and your kids forever. Ask for their participation. Include them in the planning of the event. When I was a child my family always made a big deal about my birthday (which happens to be Lincoln's Birthday—a school holiday in those days, to boot), the major Jewish holidays, and Mother's and Father's days. Everyone in my extended family—grandparents, aunts, uncles, cousins—got together to eat a fabulous meal and catch up with one another. Even my uncles who lived some distance from us came into town, which was always a special treat.

If your family is not close by, or you don't have one you feel comfortable with, you can always create a family atmosphere with friends. You can actually choose your family. Traditions are just as deep and satisfying with friends as they are with blood relatives—sometimes more so.

$\mathcal{D}$ay nine   Be a role model. Do you ever wish that your sister would take your advice about how she treats your mother, or your brother would not care so much about making money and spend more time with his kids? Well, you can help act on these desires by being a role model. Forget about giving advice, which is usually unsolicited and not well received. The best way to influence someone else is to work on yourself.

Be the way you would like others to be. If you feel you are not appreciated enough by your family, appreciate them more. If you don't think your friends call you often enough, call them more often and suggest a time and place to get together. Sometimes you won't see results immediately, and you might give up just before you realize the fruits of your intention.

Deciding to be a role model brings you love in incalculable ways. People will be attracted to you, will look to you, will intuitively recognize your sensitivity and healthy integration. And you'll be kept on your toes. You will be compelled to look for ways to be better, to learn more, to develop yourself beyond your present level of skills, to act in ways that will truly make a difference, both in your life and in the lives of those closest to you.

Day ten   Spend a day with your in-laws. Difficulties with in-laws, which are not, unfortunately, always a myth, come mostly from mutual suspicion and distrust that can only be remedied through communication and contact. Start the process. See your in-laws first as people who have their own needs and ways of doing things that may be completely different from your own. Discuss your similarities and also your differences, but try to do this in a loose, casual atmosphere. It's best to pick neutral territory. It's sometimes easier to be real and honest in a public place than to sit around the fireplace in your in-laws' living room staring straight ahead.

If you and your in-laws come from completely different cultures—either religiously, racially, or ethnically—see if you can explore the characteristics of your respective cultures. Even if you feel your in-laws are set in their ways and are having a hard time accepting you, don't give up. Here's an opportunity to show how well you can inspire confidence in people whom you may not know very well but whose support, understanding, and love make a big difference in the quality of your marriage. You may certainly get by with distant or cold relations with your in-laws, but life is so much easier when you truly like each other.

There are a variety of things to talk about. You can start with your kids, if you have any. You can talk about their recollections of your spouse. Ask to see some baby pictures, or find out what he or she was like as a child. Parents usually love to talk about their kids, even if they are grown and married. Let your in-laws know that you are interested in them, that they matter to you, that you didn't just marry their son but intend to merge two families together to create a richer life.

Day eleven   Give someone in your family a thoughtful gift. Or if you're feeling particularly ambitious, choose more than one relative and spend the day buying things for them.

The gifts do not have to be expensive. In fact, you don't have to purchase every one of them. Some may be things you already have and want to give to a family member. Some may be items you make, something that comes out of your creative energy, while others may be toys, trinkets, or other articles that are store-bought. Regardless of where the gift comes from, make sure it is special, that it is tailored to each person in a way that he or she would truly appreciate. Remember, it's not the cost, it's the thought and the appropriateness that matter.

What would your mother like to have today? Maybe it's merely a bouquet or a new plant that she would want to add to the garden in which she takes so much pride. How about your father-in-law? Since he's always talking about political matters, maybe a biography of a past president would be the right thing, or a subscription to a periodical that covers current events.

What about your kids? I'm sure you know just what they would like, since it's likely that they've been telling you for weeks or maybe months. Get it for them. Whether it's a new pair of sneakers or a lamp for the desk in your daughter's room, include it on your list and present it to her when she least expects it, maybe when she comes home from school today.

And then there is your husband, wife, or partner. Write a love note if no particular item comes to mind. Or make him breakfast and serve it to him in bed with a single flower and a bright smile. When you give someone a gift, even if it's a person you see every day and with whom you constantly interact, you demonstrate in yet another way how much he or she means to you, that you are thinking about her, that you want to please her. Even someone who isn't particularly fond of gifts would be delighted by the right surprise. Think this idea through and act on your love with a well-placed gift.

Day twelve   Develop a vision for your family. It amazes me how many times I run into people who have a crystal-clear idea of where they want their lives, and especially their careers, to go but don't give more than a passing thought to what they want from their family lives. "As long as my kids are safe and not into drugs" to me is not enough of a vision. There are many other issues that may go unaddressed without a family vision.

A family vision is simply the *kind* of life you want to live. Without my being aware of it at the time, my parents' vision was one of advancement and security. Education was seen as the ticket to ample income using brainpower instead of back power. That was fundamentally the vision. It was implicit in every decision that came up as a family unit. Nothing would be sacrificed as long as it was for education and contributed to learning and the development of our minds.

What is your vision for your family? What do you want your children to have as a result of being part of your particular constellation? Do you want your kids to be financially well off, to enjoy their work, to have harmonious relationships with the people around them, to love well, to be happy? There is an infinite number of ways to put together your vision, and of course consulting your kids if they are old enough to understand what you are talking about is valuable and also part of a vision of inclusiveness, of collegiality, of decision by consensus rather than fiat.

My wife and I have a vision for our family, and we turn to it when we consider the big questions every family faces. Education is important for our kids. Even though our children are small, we want them to be in an environment that nurtures and encourages their uniqueness, creativity, and emotional expression, that values them as individuals. Travel, cultural diversity, and experience are also important. Book learning is to be balanced with life learning. Enjoying one's work and prosperity is valued more than earning an income at the expense of integrity or time together as a family. We would rather have a smaller house and play more together than have a bigger house and work longer hours.

Develop your vision. See yourself living a life that appeals to you, and at the right time you will see the manifestation of your goal. The clearer your vision—the more inclined you are to talk about what's important to you—the more likely you are to transform your vision into reality.

Day thirteen   Apologize for something. Build a bridge to a relative by admitting a mistake and letting him or her know you understand his or her feelings.

It doesn't even have to be something you've done recently. It could be from years ago, when you were a child, or something that the person to whom you are going to apologize has long forgotten. Bring up something you said or did and say you're sorry about it, that you want to make amends simply by recognizing your mistake or insensitivity. Express how you felt during the incident, or better yet, how you feel in the moment you are apologizing.

Offering someone an apology, even for a faux pas committed long ago, makes you into a loving person, a person whose pride does not get in the way of admitting mistakes. If you have to make a choice between being loving or being right, choose to be loving.

I recently received a call from a woman who worked for me many years ago. I hadn't spoken to her in the intervening time, and she called to apologize for an incident that had occurred while we worked together. The call shocked me, not only because I had completely forgotten the incident, but also because this woman had the courage, after so much time had passed, to be vulnerable and admit her faults.

When you apologize, you tell the world that the most important thing in your life is the desire to reach out, to connect, to obliterate any difference between you and someone you care about.

Day fourteen Confront a family member. Just as there is sometimes a need to make amends through a well-placed apology, there is also occasionally the need to confront someone in order to get at something that is driving a wedge between you and that person. A confrontation does not have to be nasty or vindictive, or even bitter or angry. It only needs to be direct and loving. Keep in mind that in life conflict is inevitable, but resentment and violence are not. In fact, the way to avoid violent confrontations is to deal with the issue when it first arises, or when it continues long enough to merit some kind of airing.

When you confront this family member, talk about how you feel. Raise the issue not to blame her for her behavior but to alert her to the effect she is having on you. At that point, she has the choice of changing, or telling you that you must accept what she does because she will not change. But at least you have informed her that a choice has to be made.

Avoid saying, "You always" or "You never." Confine what you say to statements about your own feelings. To your partner you may say, "I am sad when you talk about how great your life was before you met me," or "I feel invisible and uncared for when you look at other women in restaurants. I would feel loved and respected if you were more attentive to me." You may say to your mother, "When you tell me what to eat and how to run my life, I feel insecure about my own decisions, and that makes me angry. I want to feel more in control. I ask you please to respect me as an adult and not give me advice unless I ask for it."

See that your confrontation is honest, loving, specific, and undertaken with the idea that the other person will respect you more than he or she now does.

Day fifteen See your kids as people, not just kids. If you don't have children, then see your nieces and nephews as people, or your neighbor's or friend's kids as people.

So often parents relate to their children in a one-dimensional way, as a parent to a child. Broaden your role. Go beyond the notion of caretaker and see yourself as a mentor, or friend, or confidant, as one who gently guides your children toward choices that make sense for them because you see them as individuals rather than as "kids." Honor their uniqueness, their singularity, the sense that what may work for you may not work for them; pay careful attention to their special requirements so that they are not forced by subtle pressure or coercion to be people they are not.

The whole point of this is to prepare your kids to be

adults, to understand that your relationship with them is incomparable and that other people will not necessarily see them as you do. Learn to relate to them in different ways. Be their friend at times, their confidant at others. Be vulnerable with them so they will not put you on a pedestal, so later in life they can relate to you without having to first put aside their feelings that you are omnipotent.

Value their opinions, especially about matters that concern them. Even small children have an innate sense of what they need, and all too often their requests are ignored in favor of "I know what's best for you, I'm your mommy," or "I don't care what Daddy does. When you are with Grandpa we'll do it this way." Kids are smart. They often know what works for them even when it seems impossible that they do. If you see them as people and not just kids, if you value them as individuals, if you endeavor at all times to learn what they want from you, then you will be doing all you can to be a positive influence in their lives, to be a role model they will look to over and over again.

The Path
of Healing and
Wholeness

As a professional matchmaker, I hear repeatedly the qualities people desire in a partner. Almost everyone says that he or she is looking for someone who is vital and fit, who knows how to take care of himself and doesn't abuse his body with cigarettes, alcohol, or excessive eating.

By no means do I mean to suggest that people who are unfit, ill, or infirm cannot love, or be attractive and desirable. In fact, many people who suffer from serious maladies are the most loving, caring, and understanding people I have known. But this fact illuminates a point about health and healing—namely, what it is and what it isn't.

Most people think that good health means perfect health, that nothing hurts and everything functions as it was intended to and there are no apparent symptoms of distress or disease. That's not the case for me. Good health and fitness mean that you are aware of your own body, which includes mind and spirit, that you have taken control of your own healing as much as possible. Even if you are enduring a terminal illness, you have choices. When a woman I had participated in a group with got cancer, I witnessed her dealing with the last year of her life. Her body was being eaten away by the treatments to which she had agreed, but her mind and spirit remained healthy and intact, and she was an inspiration to everyone around her.

The same standard applies to "healthy" people. Their bodies may be strong, but their minds and spirits may be weak and infirm. They may pollute their systems with addictive poisons, maintain ignorant prejudices, conduct themselves in a selfish, rude, or insensitive manner, or erroneously believe that their superficially good health will protect them from their inability to connect with either themselves or others. They are mistaken. Healthy people possess the ability to love, to extend themselves, to express affection and other emotions, to forgive. It is not merely a condition of all of one's body parts and functions operating without distress. *Good health is a psychological and emotional, as well as a physical, state.* It is concerned with what can't be immediately seen or felt—for instance, kindness, humanitarian feeling, and empathy—as well as what can be.

In my experience, people who love most deeply and fully are people who are healthy. They may have their occasional aches and pains, but for the most part they are in touch with their bodies. They are fully acquainted not only with their personalities but with their own personal ecosystems as well.

They understand the connection between their

physical selves and the choices they make in life, the people with whom they choose to associate, and how they express their love, and they are in turn rewarded consistently by life. They are blessed with healthy relationships, warm and loving friends, and supportive and nurturing family members. They also realize that they are not passive participants in this process, that they do not come to possess such abundance through "luck" but through their own diligent efforts to know themselves, to honor and respect their bodies, to create good health and healing through mindful attention to what is best in life, and to avoid but also to forgive themselves for what is not.

Somehow, in love, the separation between inner and outer fades as you get deeper and deeper into it. The way you relate to your own body is ultimately the way you relate to *every* body. It works both ways. You can learn to develop healthy habits through your loving associations with others, or you can learn to love more fully and directly by listening to what your own body is telling you. Everything you need to know about love can be discovered within your own person. It is not to be found in your lover's eyes but in your own.

Day one Get body work done. This could mean a massage, a facial, or any other type of gentle ministration. The particular type doesn't matter. What does is the awareness you bring to your own physical being, the attention you provide your body as someone administers to you.

You can do yoga, which involves stretching gently and breathing deeply, or make a special trip to a spa and partake of any of a number of alternatives. You can immerse yourself in a mud bath, allow yourself to be placed in a samadhi tank or box that will warm you, or get into a hot tub, Jacuzzi, sauna, or steam room. Any of these will alter your body's environment enough to make you aware of how you feel. And usually, after any of these treatments—or all of them, for that matter—you'll feel better.

Let go of all your cares, worries, frustrations, and anxieties, as you feel the strong and knowing hands work over your muscles and tender spots. Let your body worker know just the way you like your massage. If you want him or her to work deeply, mention this. If there are particular places in your body where you hold stress, like your neck, shoulders, back, or abdomen, have your masseuse or masseur concentrate on those areas. The time on the massage table is your time. Make the most of it.

Breathe deeply as you feel someone else's fingers, hands, or elbows work through your tight spots. Let go of control. Feel the tension flee from your limbs and torso as the gentle pressure performs its magic. To really get the full benefit of the body work, make sure your massage lasts at least an hour. If you can manage ninety minutes, you'll really notice the difference.

When your session is complete, lie on the table in silence for a few minutes. Notice the way your body feels without the tension, the accumulated stress of your daily life. Then get up slowly, dress, thank yourself for this wonderful indulgence, and continue with the day.

$\mathcal{D}$ay two   Fulfill your *partner's* health needs. This may be trickier and somewhat more difficult than fulfilling your own, but with time, care, and attention, it certainly can be done.

Each of us has his or her own way of dealing with our health and healing, whether we are well or suffering from an illness. Find out what your partner requires. In fact, it's a good idea to know what all your family members' needs are when they are not feeling well. So much of good health, and recovery in the event of sickness, is emotional and psychological that it's important to know what is required of you to be of maximum benefit to someone close.

Some people like to have extra attention paid to them when they are not feeling well, while others want to go about their business as if everything were normal. And just because you handle illness or discomfort a certain way doesn't mean your partner does, so you've got to ask, to make sure you are fulfilling his or her desires, and not a projection of your own.

Does your partner have low back pain? See if you can ease his burden by massaging the area, setting up a comfortable spot in the living room, or helping him get up or lie down. Is it important for someone close to you to exercise every day? Help fulfill her health needs by cheerfully suggesting a walk, rather than lecturing her about not heeding the warnings of her physician.

You may have to call the doctor, get aspirin, or administer a balm or salve. Or you may have to leave temporarily while your husband, wife, partner, or special friend tries to recover by sleeping. Offer to give whatever help your partner asks of you. And keep in mind that often when people are feeling low, they will not think to ask for help. They want it but cannot articulate it. Keep asking. And if your partner puts you off by continually telling you that everything is fine, when you can plainly see that it is not, then take things a step further and make suggestions. "Shall I bring you a cup of tea and a piece of toast, my dear?" or "Would you like me to run a hot bath for you, sweetheart?"

And don't forget about a nurturing hug and kiss. Sometimes that's all a person needs to feel better in that moment, regardless of the severity of the illness. Remember to keep this option open at all times.

Day three   Move your body. You don't even have to call it exercise if you have developed an aversion to the word. You can be like Alfred Kahn, an economic adviser to President Carter, who refused in testimony before Congress to say the word "depression." He called it a banana. Call exercise a pineapple if you want, just do it.

If you haven't pushed your body since you were in high school, start slowly, and make sure you check in first with your doctor. If you get the green light, even the slightest activity will help. Start out by walking twenty minutes a day three times a week, then gradually after a few weeks increase both the duration and the frequency of your walks. And I'm not talking about a casual stroll through your neighborhood during which you stop and chat with your friends and smell each new flower. I mean a vigorous jaunt, one that makes you feel your heart rate increase.

If walking doesn't do it for you, try swimming, or get on a bicycle and pedal around a local park. Or if your budget permits, buy a treadmill or StairMaster, or join a gym and work out regularly. Learn to ski. Cross-country skiing is an especially good workout, as is running, if your knees and back can take the wear and tear. Remember to get athletic shoes that will absorb the impact, and try to run on softer surfaces, such as a track or dirt path. Avoid concrete.

Everyone agrees that exercise is a key to good health. So many of our modern-day ailments—both physical and mental—result from the fact that we are sedentary, that we sit at a desk for eight hours or more a day and allow our muscles to deteriorate through lack of use. And then our metabolism reacts by encouraging us to eat more and unhealthfully, and then our overeating and bad diet make exercise that much more unpalatable.

If you already exercise, congratulate yourself for your discipline and good sense, and make sure you're not over-doing it. Remember, the objective is balance, not excess.

Day four Get lots of fresh air. Get out into the open, away from offices and other rooms that have recycled air, where the windows don't open and you can only guess what it's like outside. Experience the real thing. Go outdoors.

When you're out on the street, or away from the city in a forest, or in the mountains, or on the beach, take as many deep breaths as you can to experience the feeling of fresh air. Whether it's raining or snowing, or it's a glori-ously sunny day, fill up your lungs with one of life's indis-pensable elements—oxygen. Revel in it the way a small child delights in a trip to the toy store.

If time permits, take a hike during your lunch break, or wait for the weekend and bring your kids or someone else's kids along. You can invite a friend and suggest that you make the purpose of your day the overabsorption of fresh air. Come up with creative ways to do this. Stop every so often and take fifty deep breaths. Be aware of your breathing—what it feels like, what it sounds like, how comfortable you are with it. While you obviously must breathe to live, see if you can concentrate on it as never before, as you repeatedly fill your lungs with the fruits of photosynthesis. Thank trees and the other plant life you encounter for making your life not only possible but enjoyable.

Make fresh air a regular part of your daily life. Unless you were fasting, you wouldn't think of going a single day without eating, would you? Put fresh air in the same category, and try to combine it with vigorous movement.

Day five   Express your feelings. So much of good health, and hence of a loving life, is being able to get out what's on your mind and in your heart. And it doesn't have to be negative. Suppressing a positive or loving feeling can be just as unhealthy as keeping down a resentful or angry one.

As a relationship counselor, it amazes me every time I see a couple that concocts elaborate strategies to avoid dealing with the feelings they have for each other. It's as if they've decided that expressing anything strong or passionate will upset some delicate balance of equanimity that exists between them. This path leads to difficulty. It's important to learn to articulate what's there, to create a relationship of dynamic tension by expressing what's going on.

Do you feel terrible when your partner forgets to acknowledge your birthday? Let her know. Are you beginning to resent the little digs that keep coming out of the mouth of a friend at inopportune times? Tell him about it. If you feel you can't because he or she will react negatively and end the relationship, then you don't have a healthy one right now.

When you communicate what you feel, you must be gentle, open, and direct. Avoid defensiveness or blame. Remember, the point of this is to begin the process of dispelling your anger. If you express your feelings in a responsible, heartfelt manner, without name calling, guilt-tripping, or melodrama, you improve a hundredfold the chances of the other person's hearing you, which is your objective in all this, of course.

But keep in mind also that the primary purpose in taking this step is to keep your health in equilibrium, to prevent the buildup of physical or emotional toxins. This is why so many people turn to therapy or counseling, because they cannot reveal what is most significant to them, living instead in a world of superficialities that only mask reality. If you can express yourself directly, honestly, and also with kindness and not rancor, then you will find the world a more loving place, and you will be surrounded with loving people, even if there are only a few of them.

Day six   Clean out your body. Don't let it become a repository for more toxins than is absolutely necessary. Spend a day taking in substances that are as pure as possible, with few contaminants or chemicals. If this day turns out to be pleasurable, make a habit of this, and after a while, see if you notice any difference in your mood, disposition, energy level, or appearance.

For starters, give up the most obvious culprits, if they have become a habit with you—tobacco, caffeine, or alcohol. Even if you are an occasional user, do without for a day or a week, just to see what it feels like. Even such tasty indulgences as caffè latte or cappuccino, or the extra-dry martini at the end of the day, can build up toxins in your body, altering your delicate balance in a way that can be harmful to you.

Ridding your body of pollutants sends a message to yourself, to the world, and to everyone around you. Besides the physiological benefits, such as keeping in balance the delicate structure of natural stimulants and depressants that make you feel as physically good as possible, you positively affect your psychology and emotional life as well. You'll be able to be more open to a loving life. Your reactions to people and events will not be viewed through the lens of a chemically induced state that may not allow you to experience the world as it is.

Taking the opportunity to rid yourself of habits that you know do not serve you can become a metaphor for other areas of your life. Often, a new path in love begins with small changes that can transform themselves into big ones. When you clean out your body, you feel better—physically, mentally, emotionally—and when you feel better you love more deeply and directly. Order herb tea, juice, or mineral water instead of coffee or an alcoholic drink. Or call a friend and talk to him or her every time you feel the urge to reach for a cigarette.

Healthy, loving habits can become just as ingrained as damaging ones. Start forming them today.

Day seven Balance your activities. It's best to start with the premise that there is time for everything, that nothing need be sacrificed for anything else. Obviously, you must make some choices, but if you have as your life goal the notion of balance, then you will choose wisely. It just doesn't make sense to spend twice as much time as you need to working and not have a social life, or devote too much time to socializing and not enough to projects that reflect your creativity.

It makes sense to balance your work schedule so you don't fall victim to what the Japanese call *karoshi*—death from overwork. There are severe negative consequences from spending too much time at the office in an unbalanced manner for long periods—like fatigue, difficulty forming other kinds of relationships, an inability to relax, viewing life through the prism of work—and the best way to ensure that this doesn't happen to you is to make time for other activities.

Work, play, exercise, service to others, and an active, nurturing love and social life are the basics. Each person's requirements are obviously different, and it may take a while to experiment with various combinations, but if you have balance in mind, your health will reflect this attitude. Too much of any one thing isn't good for you. You may spend certain periods of your life working, and others resting, and still others exercising. That's fine. What's important is to look at the long haul, to see your life as a marathon stretched out before you, in equilibrium, doing everything you can in the right measure.

Day eight   Learn to relax. This is perhaps the most difficult task we modern people face. Is your life a constant struggle? Are you always at the ready, constantly prepared to face your boss, your wife, or that saber-toothed tiger that's about to come over the hill and threaten you? Does this sound like your life? If it does, why not take the time today to learn how to relax.

Relaxation involves a variety of factors. The first is your breathing. Pay attention to how fully and how often you breathe. If you learn to take deep breaths, you'll find yourself less inclined to be tense. Next, slow down. There's certainly not as much rush to do whatever you have to do as you think there is. If you find yourself always rushing, then you're either overcommitted or not managing your day to serve you. Reexamine how much you've taken on, or what you're spending time doing.

Take your time with everything you do. Be present with whatever you're involved with by committing your mind, body, and spirit to each moment. Spend time with people you love, with those who make you feel happy. If this means your partner and your kids, play with them. Interact on a regular basis and make this a part of your daily life. If you are single and don't have any kids, get together with special friends or acquaintances with whom you can enjoy leisure time. Share yourself. Attend a performance or make a meal. Go bowling, visit a museum, or explore a flea market together. Take advantage of activities that don't require much money.

Finally, listen to your body. If it tells you to slow down, slow down. Give yourself time off for good behavior—as often as you feel the desire. If that's a lot, then you probably need it. If you're sitting around doing very little and you want to pick up the pace a bit, to take some initiative and reach out, do that as well.

*D*ay nine   Take control of your own health and healing. Don't give them up to anyone. Of all the people in the world—doctors and relatives included—you know what's best for you. Trust yourself. Be in charge of your well-being.

This doesn't mean deliberately disregarding the opinion of others, including the doctor or other health practitioners with whom you may be in contact. It only means that you are the one calling the shots, that ultimately all decisions about staying well or healthy, or getting well or healthy, are made by you. Everyone else is an adviser. If you have a problem and are being told to undergo a certain procedure, you can get a second opinion, or a third if it's warranted. You can also try an alternative method like chiropractic, acupuncture, or homeopathy if you feel you want to treat the origins of your condition.

Ask questions. If you're having trouble with your vision, ask your doctor what he or she thinks is the cause. How frequently is this condition seen in a person your age? What are the chances that your eyes will get better on their own? Is there someone who specializes in these cases to whom you can be referred? Play an active role in your recovery. You can direct it by focusing your energy and your attention on getting well, on making wellness a top priority in your life.

Use the same approach with medical insurance companies, which can be intimidating and bewildering. Ask for clarification, for bills, notices, and explanations for the differences between what your doctor and your insurer say. So often, healing comes from knowing what is, rather than speculating on what could be. Demonstrate to people with whom you deal that you are an individual and you require individual attention, not a cookie-cutter approach to your situation.

Every problem—from the smallest to the largest, from a hangnail to heart disease—calls out for your attention. The one person who ought to be directing the course of your health or recovery is you. Be the leader. Show the people with whom you interact that you have the desire to find out how well or how ill you really are, and the intention to do whatever it takes to get well again.

$\mathcal{D}$ay ten   Practice yoga. Find out about a nearby instructor who teaches a class, or go to your local college or university and make inquiries or look at bulletin boards for notices. Another way to practice yoga is to buy a videotape. That way you can do it anytime you want to in your own living room or bedroom, although it's often helpful to learn with a teacher who can make suggestions to correct your positions. Or you can read a book.

The practice of yoga will gently and slowly improve your health, wellness, and ability to heal, regardless of your body's present condition. Keep in mind that this is not a competitive exercise, and the effects are very subtle. But breathing and stretching in tandem, moving every muscle, every limb, will carry positive messages to the many internal systems your body employs to balance and center yourself. Your being will learn a way of keeping healthy that has been practiced for thousands of years, integrating acute body awareness and attention to your Higher Self.

There are many different types of yoga being taught today by people who are trained and have integrity. Find out more about them before you commit yourself to a class. And try to stick with your practice long enough to get used to this new routine. It might take a while to realize the gains you are making without the immediate benefit of the jumping jacks, leg kicks, sweat, and loud, pulsating rock music so frequently associated with aerobics and other more vigorous exercises.

When you start your practice, see if you can sustain a regular discipline. It's better to go two times per week for an extended period of time than to practice every day for a month, burn out, and then give up. Of course, the more you practice the more benefits you'll realize, but it's also true that the longer you practice the greater the benefit as well. Get into a rhythm. Make sure you like the way your teacher instructs you, that her suggestions are gentle and supportive, and that she recognizes the spiritual nature of yoga.

At the conclusion of each session, lie on your back in a peaceful and relaxed manner, known as the corpse position, slowing down from your series of stretches, feeling the full relaxed glow of the gentle workout you gave your body, rather like giving it a gift.

Day eleven   Scream. Take the opportunity today or—if you find this method of releasing tension appeals to you—every day to let out whatever you are keeping inside and may have kept inside for a long period of time, maybe years. If you can't find a place to do this because someone will hear you and think you have gone off the deep end, try the shower. Or scream into a pillow. That will allow you the full benefit of this release without any of the drawbacks. You can let your tension out safely and securely and walk away from this activity feeling emotionally refreshed and cleansed.

Encountering the Soul Through the Invisible World

When I was young, there was an advertising campaign that touted 7UP as the un-Cola. Evidence indicates that there is a world out there, infinitely larger and more mysterious than the world we see every day, that can be called the Unseen. And because we don't see it and can't quantify or dissect it or observe it under a microscope, that doesn't mean this world doesn't exist, or that it cannot be encountered, or that it doesn't have great importance for our everyday lives.

Human beings have made reference to this world since the beginning of time. This is the world of our ultimate questions: What is life? What is death? How do we know what we know? What is meaning? And finally, what is love?

The seen world is the material world, the tip of the iceberg of reality. But it is your relationship to what you can't see—guided by your faith—that ultimately governs the quality of your entire life. You will probably find it difficult to sustain deep, abiding love without some kind of spiritual component in your life, because love is fundamentally irrational. It is not material. It partakes of the divine, which is part of the world we can't see. It doesn't matter what you call your deity. It can be called anything. And it likewise doesn't matter what form it takes, whether it is masculine, feminine, or neither, whether it pervades everything or is removed and detached. It is still there.

Ultimately you cannot name it, because language is an aspect of the Seen, the material. And the Invisible World has only a casual relationship to religion, which is merely the institutional manifestation of this more primal, subconscious, spiritual realm. I've known "religious" people who were doctrinaire but didn't understand the first thing about reverence for the divine, and "spiritual" people who hadn't seen the inside of a church or synagogue in years but in whom I would entrust my very existence, and that of my family.

People who have a healthy relationship with the Invisible World know how to love, because they recognize that love itself is ultimately a leap of faith, a way of connecting with the source of all power, with the divine, the miraculous. Human love is only one small—but significant—reflection of the Invisible World. It reminds us that this world truly exists. Most of the time the Invisible World cannot be seen, but it certainly can be known. You know it when you nurture something, whether it's a plant or an idea, or a child you are entrusted with raising. You know it when something inside tells you to move ahead, pull back, or just wait for a moment, regardless of what the plus and minus sides of the ledger sheet say. And you know it for certain when you are sleeping, when a great, vast, seemingly incomprehensible world that exists somewhere inside you suddenly awakens and introduces you to parts of yourself that lie dormant while you are conscious.

My life unfolded radically when I realized that my own intelligence was limited, that it could not solve every problem—either in my own life or in the world—and that it didn't need to. Accepting the idea that there is a greater intelligence apart from and beyond my own, but of which mine partakes, convinces me that the loving relationships with the people and the possibilities in my life are but a reflection of love itself. And this is something the Invisible World chooses to reveal to me, to remind me of its existence.

Day one Practice humility. This does not mean prostrating yourself in the face of a greater power, or considering yourself less than anybody or anything else. Humility is not about feeling insecure, powerless, or timid. It is about proportion, about understanding your role. If you are humble, you proceed through life with the understanding that what you know could be altered by circumstances, events, ideas, contact with something unexpected, or a relationship with a lover or family member that takes your world right out from under you.

Humility is living life—speaking, acting, thinking, being—with the understanding that you are an open book, that if there is any power before which you are bowing, it is the existence of the invisible. It is living in deference to it, in deference to everything before you. It is seeing the value in all things, without regard to place or position. It is deeming holy everything—a tear, a smile, a swarm of bees, the love you feel for your partner, your children, or your family, and the idea of life itself.

Humility is the true state of nature and the Invisible World. The sturdy oak tree is cut down by a strong wind while the lowly grass survives. The grass is eaten by a grazing cow as the oak tree watches in silent testimony. The mighty wind is stirred and then calmed by the perpetual turning of the earth. All is humble.

If you practice humility, if you go about your business as lightly as you can, you know love. You understand the ability to connect because your probes are gentle and invite response. They are direct, but they are also yielding. Love is humility, the sense of not knowing and therefore treading lightly, as if life were a sheet of thin ice that would crack under the weight of too much emphasis.

Day two   Think about your Higher Self. First, let go of the part of you that you show the world every day, the part that people expect to see. This could even include the part that *you* expect to see. Forget about all your roles, your relationship to the outside, to the world of money, possessions, success, relationships, and commitments. For as long as you can—even for an hour—shed all this and focus on the real you.

Sit quietly and comfortably by a roaring fire, or if the weather permits, take a walk in a peaceful setting and concentrate on the person you are without these external trappings. What would your life look like if you didn't have them? Who would you be? What would you think about? What would occupy your attention, your time? Who would be in your heart?

Answers and information are not what you're looking for. Even the questions that may arise are not important. What you want to conjure up is feeling, pure intelligence, the kind that is not limited by rational thinking, that has no name. Stay with this a while longer. Even if you draw a blank, see that as the first step to finding out more about what's inside you. Plan to engage in this activity again soon, for a longer period of time.

When you think about your Higher Self, you signal the Invisible World to enter your life. For a moment, you are living at a more sublime level, your entire being radiating with energy that transcends material existence. It's not that the everyday isn't important—it most certainly is. It's just that life also includes its complement—the higher part of you, the part that supersedes time and space and lives in a kind of eternity you glimpse from time to time and would know better if you deliberately focused on it.

Make the effort to become acquainted with your Higher Self. It's like any other relationship. The more time you devote to it, the more it grows.

Day three Be on the lookout for angels. You've probably heard about heavenly spirits all your life. Whether you first read about or saw murals of them in a religious context, or learned about them in school when you studied the Middle Ages or Renaissance, or apply the term to a cute child or dear friend, or root for a Southern California baseball team, chances are you have some familiarity with the term. See if you can detect an angel or two in your own life.

Where do you think you'd find one? Would you look in your car, under your desk at the office, or on top of the television? Perhaps you would look for an angel near a church. Perhaps not. Maybe there's an angel staying close to an infant you know, protecting him or her from other, more mischievous spirits.

What would you do if you actually saw an angel? What do you think it would look like? People in the Middle Ages certainly had an idea—a small, round, cherubic face and body, childlike and adultlike at the same time, sometimes blowing a horn. Why do you think these people depicted angels this way? Was it because they actually saw them? Or imagined them? What role do you think angels played in their lives? Could they play a role in your life?

If you think about angels, whether you ever actually see any or merely contemplate them, this thought puts you in touch with the Invisible World, even if it's only in your mind, or in your heart, which is real enough. And if you actually saw an angel, or felt its presence, what would you do? Would you ask it something? Recoil in terror, as the poet Rilke did? Just stand there? What kind of guidance would you ask for right now?

It's important to have these questions in mind. You never know when you're going to meet an angel.

Day four   Imagine heaven. Immerse yourself in the idea of Nirvana, Paradise, Eden, Valhalla. Think of how many names the different cultures of the planet have for this place—a world in which pain is abolished, a world that knows no right and wrong, that is not saddled with the responsibility of knowledge.

What is your idea of heaven? Is it a place where people follow your wishes, every dish you cook comes out perfectly, deer don't eat your flowers, barking dogs don't exist? Or is your idea of heaven a place where everyone in the world eats well and has a roof over his head every night, where people respect one another, where no guns and weapons of any kind exist, and swords have been beaten into plowshares?

Is your idea of heaven a place where men and women think about others, where integrity is more than just a word, where leaders are wise and don't just consider their own political careers? Or is it more personal, a place where your pain—either physical or emotional—is gone, where your relations with your family members are smooth and easy, where those close by listen and pay attention to you, and you to them? Is that your idea of heaven?

I know my idea of heaven. It has to do with love. All the people—past, present, and future—whom I have or will have loved or who have or will have ever loved me are together in one place, and all my feelings for them are present and powerful. This place contains my family, my dear friends, close relatives who have passed on, former lovers at the apex of our feelings, and even girls with whom I was infatuated in elementary school. Everyone would meet, and we would talk and exchange knowing glances of love and regard, and no one would have any agenda other than the simple pleasure of being in one another's pres-

You can do your praying in a traditional house of worship, alone, or together with a friend in your home. You can be silent or pray out loud. What matters is your intention. Really concentrate on what you have in mind. Spend a certain amount of time each day asking God, Allah, Jesus, or the Universe to bring you a fit body, better connections with Mom and Dad, or your close friend's recovery.

Ask humbly, respectfully, and unequivocally. Act as if there really is a universal switchboard that hears all requests for miracles and acts on them based on the sincerity, worthiness, and earnestness of the request and the requester. Pray and wait. Wait and pray. In some cases, that's all you can do.

Day seven   Chant. Tap into another energy source. Find out about some traditional religious chants, or make up your own. They can be in English or in any other language. Each of the world's religions has chants that have been passed from generation to generation. These enable people to make contact with divinities that help us live more closely with universal forces that are not seen, and not usually accessed.

All traditional cultures chant. Buddhists chant. Native Americans chant. Catholics chant. Jews chant. Moslems chant. Now you can chant. Pick out a word, string of words, or sentence, and repeat it. When I was a graduate student, studying in London in 1975, I met a wonderful wise man from Sri Lanka in the reading room of the British Museum. We became friendly and he gave me a Hindu chant to turn to whenever I needed help. I'll share it with you: "Om taré, tut taré, thuré, svahak" (pronounced *Ohm tar-ay tuht tar-ay tuhr-ay zva-hahk*). Keep saying this over and over again, until you just can't say it any longer. You'll feel closer to the divine.

I've also participated in rhythmic, melodious chants with hundreds of people dancing in a circle, intoning the same phrases thousands of times for several hours, until all my senses began to blend and I couldn't distinguish between sight and sound, and my words no longer belonged exclusively to me but became everyone else's as well.

If you really want to get in touch with the Invisible World, you can do so by chanting on a regular basis. You can do this by yourself at home (I wouldn't recommend that you chant at the airport) or with others. Try an experiment. Spend the next week chanting each day for five minutes. You can chant in the shower. Just repeat the same line over and over again and see what happens. And whenever you need some assistance from an unseen source, remember the chant I've given you.

Day eight   Have a discussion about death. Select someone with whom you feel completely comfortable and whose opinion you value, and allow yourself the opportunity to air your feelings. Make sure the person you choose—your father, partner, son or daughter, friend, grandmother—understands you in a most fundamental way, sees your life as precious and valuable, and has come through with loving emotional support when you needed it.

Bring up your fears and anxieties. Try to be comfortable with them. Talk about your experiences with death, what it felt like when someone close to you died, how the people around you reacted. Talk about how your particular culture reacts to death and how other cultures react. Try to get at what is so frightening about death, why we talk about it only fleetingly, tentatively, with great reluctance and trepidation. Is the fear of death the fear of the pain of death? The nothingness of death? The unknowingness of death?

See if in preparation for this discussion you can read what some of the great minds of our culture have written about this subject. See what Jung thought about death, or Socrates, or Jesus, or Martin Luther King. Discuss the many words we use to express death. When I was a kid, using slang, I said "croaked." The medical profession uses "expire" or "demise," terms that sound as clinical as they are. The term that I prefer at this point in my life is "passed on," which for me connotes continuation. It means that life hasn't ended, it has merely entered a different phase. "Passed away," a term my family uses, means to me that someone is no longer accessible. "Died" is so final, so typical of our materialist culture.

Try to work through your anxieties by discussing them with your friend and listening to what he or she has to say. Ask questions. Work toward a comfortable position, one that makes you feel better to be alive. When you deal with your fears, they no longer have the same hold on you. And isn't death the ultimate fear, the one fear that gives life to all others?

Day nine   Submit yourself to the divine. Here's the scenario. There is a force, about which I've been speaking; this force exists in a world that's invisible, and because we can't see it, we don't think it's there. But it is, and some people have seen it, and written and talked about it. Because most of us haven't experienced it, we don't believe it or can't imagine it. But let's pretend it exists. This force guides every one of us toward what is good and right, and in fact it is so good and right that it goes beyond the words *good* and *right* into qualities that we can't describe. Let's call this force "perfect" or "divine."

Let's also say that the only thing that holds us back from being guided and in fact swept along by this force is our own will, our own mind-guided sense that we can "figure out" what to do, whether it's whom to sleep with, or where to work, or what to name our children, or how much money we need to earn. And all we need to do to end our tension and feel real relaxation is to forget about making decisions and let the divine intelligence decide for us. Since it has more information at its disposal, since it sees the big picture, it will be able to decide for us much better than we can decide for ourselves.

If all this sounds crazy to you, try it for just one day. If you already believe it, then continue opening yourself up even more to the divine. I'm not suggesting passivity, thinking that there is no more work to be done, that God or the universe is going to do everything for you. In fact, you may now have more work to do. You may have to get in alignment with your true nature, or Higher Self, or whatever you want to call it, and that might be the hardest work of all, since you may have to undo what you've already done and build a whole new life.

Are you interested? If you are, then recognize the divine, within you and without you, and surrender to it. Bring it directly in. Proceed with the notion that you are now guided by a higher power that knows what's best for you, like a child who depends on his mother and father to tell him what to do because he's had little experience with certain matters and requires assistance. And when you give in to this way of being, the answers will come to you, at the right time, in the right place and circumstances. Does this sound like a paradox? It is. Is this life? Yes.

Day ten   Investigate your original religion. Regardless of your faith now, whether you are a Baptist and you started out an Episcopalian, or you are a Buddhist and you were raised Roman Catholic, or you are a member of the Ba'hai faith and were born a Jew, find out about the beginnings of your first faith. Go back as far as you can. Even if religion per se has no appeal, no allure for you, do this as a purely intellectual exercise, or as a way to reach back into your roots. And of course, if you consider yourself a religious person, if you are a regular, devout churchgoer, then do this out of your love for God or whatever you call your divinity.

To a large extent, the information you uncover will depend on the questions you ask. Who is the founder of your religion? From what social or economic class did he or she come? In what country or region of the world did your original faith take hold? How long has it been in existence? What did it develop in reaction to? What factors did it feel the prevailing faiths lacked?

If you ask questions like these, you will find out a lot about your original faith, and about yourself, or if you are not particularly religious or have taken on another faith, your ancestors. But you can ask other questions. What does your faith say about life? About death? About life after death? What is truth? What is the concept of the divinity? Where did life come from? Where is it going? What is the relationship between human life and other forms of life?

What is the connection between thought and action? What is good? What is evil? Who judges?

These are the ultimate questions, the questions that religion and to a lesser extent philosophy concern themselves with. And if you look at these questions through the lens of your original faith, you will come to know yourself in a new way, through the filter of the Invisible World, through questions whose answers are only more questions.

The Cycles
of Love

When you conjure up images of the four seasons, what comes to mind is movement, a natural order we accept as a given. In spring, we see birth and blossoming; we see that nature has not deserted us but has been busily at work getting ready for a new performance. Summer brings the full realization of what spring promises. Leaves grow to their fullest and greenest. Fruits and berries ripen and provide us with much sweetness. Days are long and hot, and the intensity of summer seems a permanent presence.

But even as hot summer days and sultry nights seem never-ending, the early signs of fall appear. The leaves grow scarlet, wither, and are trampled underfoot. Cloud patterns change and reflect weather that will soon be cooler and windier. Before long fall arrives, and with it chilly nights, cold rains, and the gradual disappearance of spring's lush gifts. Winter brings retreat. Just when it seems that nature has abandoned us forever, the first buds appear and the cycle of the seasons begins anew. Winter has been but a prelude, a pause.

If you think of love in this way, you will have more of it in your life, because you will be honoring its natural rhythms. Like nature, love goes through cycles. Like anything that is alive, love develops. Even relationships that endure must change. They are never the same at the end as they were at the beginning. They have gone through the cycle of birth, maturity, decline, and death many times, as elements that were once an integral part of the landscape disappear, only to be replaced by other things.

Love will never fail you if you view it this way. You will not feel abandoned by love; even if you are lonely you will understand that the wheel of the cycle never stops, that what you lack today you will have in abundance tomorrow, and what you enjoy to the fullest right now may evaporate as soon as the wind picks up.

That is why every moment, every opportunity to express love is so important. The one thing we can be sure of is that things will change—the way you feel about your partner and he or she feels about you will evolve over time, your parents will age and pass on, your kids will grow up and move out, your friendships will constantly reflect where you are in life, the way you earn a living and how you choose to express yourself creatively will be indicative of the challenges that confront you both personally and professionally—and to accept this fact is probably the most loving act you can perform.

Love is not just romantic or sexual activities with the man or woman who is your partner. It is developing an intimate relationship with all of life, with the many aspects of existence that we encounter as we mature. It is also recognizing that every relationship—like romantic or sexual love—is always at some point in a cycle, that it is never static, that it constantly partakes of the natural order of growth and development. For this reason there is never anything to fear, except perhaps our inability or disinclination to accept responsibility for our own love and fulfillment.

Instead of feeling that love has passed us by, it is so much truer to see that, for whatever reason, it is in its winter phase. But in love, as in the seasons, spring follows winter, and all the lack, the barrenness, the dormancy will soon be but a distant memory, as the inevitable bursting forth will everywhere reign.

A NOTE FROM THE AUTHOR

One of the many pleasures of writing and publishing a book is to find out what impact it has on those who read it. I received many letters in response to my first book, *How to Be Happier Day by Day: A Year of Mindful Actions*, and would be pleased to hear from you after you've read *How to Have More Love in Your Life*. Also, if you'd like to know about talks or seminars on love in your area, send me your name, address, and phone number. Write to Alan Epstein, P.O. Box 3011, San Anselmo, CA 94979.